"Falling Together is a captivating story that serves as a testament to the power of listening to your heart and trusting the universe to deliver. Vanessa beautifully describes a spiritual journey in a modern-day context to illustrate a heartfelt example of how love always finds a way."
–Sonia Choquette
NY Times Best Selling Author

"In this compelling tale of rebuilding life and love from the bottom up, Vanessa Lin shares a touching story of her heart breaking open to create the space for true love to enter. For anyone experiencing doubt that the Universe is conspiring to bring you just what you're looking for, this book might inspire you to change your mind. It's a magical journey of faith to fulfillment!"
–Katherine Woodward Thomas
NY Times Best Selling Author of
Calling in "The One:" 7 weeks to Attract the Love of Your Life

"Inspiring and enlightening! Vanessa bravely shares her story of heartbreak and the path to true healing, tuning into the power of her own Spirit to help get her to the other side. She beautifully transforms her life and comes out stronger than ever."
–Peggy Rometo
Intuitive Expert and Author of The Little Book of Big Promises

"Vanessa brings us on a deeply personal, arduous journey of her life falling apart to falling together. Her depth, wisdom, and sweetness remind us, that no matter how life unfolds, if we choose to look deeply within ourselves and trust our intuition in the face of insurmountable odds, that a life of healing, fulfillment and empowerment lie on the other side. An inspirational journey of what happens when you trust your heart, intuition and the magic of the Universe."
–Sonia Choquette Tully
Intuitive and Best Selling Author of You Are Amazing

Falling Together:

A Tale of Believing in Your Own Magic

Based on a true story

By: Vanessa Calimag Lin

Falling Together: A Tale of Believing in Your Own Magic

Copyright © 2020 Vanessa Calimag Lin.

All Rights Reserved.

Rose Gold Publishing, LLC

Table of Contents

Prologue

In the subtle moments between sleep and lucidity, as my soul touched the edge of a blissful state of dreaming, is when I saw him clearly.

Father Rookey, once a guide to me on the earthly plane, now came to me from another realm to tell me he had cleared a path. His voice boomed and echoed dramatically, as it always had when we'd met in person. He nodded his head, and out of nowhere, he rolled out a red carpet. The scene transformed. I looked around, and we were outside of a brightly lit theater. I felt like I was invited to the opening night of a Hollywood blockbuster. Was I dressed for the occasion? He smiled and laughed his hearty laugh, and the twinkle in his eye told me that I was about to embark on a magical journey. Suddenly I was pulling up in a stretch limousine wearing a sparkly gown, dressed perfectly for the adventure of the evening. I looked out the window at the sea of people waiting for me to arrive, hearing the sounds of a crowd buzzing and seeing lights flashing, photographers snapping shots of the glamorous people outside. I felt the world bounce. My eyes shot open, realizing I was lying in bed next to my husband, and it was the middle of the night. I got up out of bed and knew what was next. It was time to tell my story.

I grabbed the journal that sat ready at my bedside, flicked on a book light that I clipped to the edge of it, and began.

This book is dedicated to my guides, both earth and heaven-bound, and most especially to my family. You are the magic that I have always sought and the reason that I write.

Acknowledgements

To my sister Charmaine, who fearlessly dove into the abyss with me head-first, as I took a downward plunge, not knowing when I would emerge. Thank you for your strength and encouragement.

To my publisher Dolly and editor Alexia, who acted as my believing eyes and held my hand as I found my way through this book.

To my four angels Johan, Zakri, Zachary "Bubba", and Lukey. You make my life magical every day.

Finally, to my husband Jeremy. Thank you for truly seeing me. I love you with all my heart.

Chapter 1: Moving Out

This was supposed to be the most joyful time of my life. I shoved my belongings into boxes haphazardly, trying to move quickly – a daunting task because my hands were swollen, and my back ached from the growing little life that swirled around inside of me. I was six months pregnant, and I had to get out of this place as soon as possible. Anxiety raced through my blood as I wondered how in the world I would possibly have a proper nursery set up for my baby before he arrived. I had so much of my own life to rearrange first.

My beloved condo was a two-bedroom, two-bathroom space with a private rooftop deck area that showed off a spectacular view of the Chicago skyline, especially at night. My husband, Dylan, and I had found it nearly five years ago. Pilsen was an artsy part of Chicago with a vibe heavily influenced by Latino culture, with coffee shops, panaderias, vintage shops, bodegas, art galleries, and amazing Mexican restaurants all within walking distance. This was the first place that we had owned together, and we had picked out every finish and every tile ourselves. I remember selecting the paint colors just after we had closed on our unit. We'd chosen a mustard-colored accent wall and used a distressing glazing technique to give it a textured look. We'd painted the rest of the living room a deep maroon, and the combination of these colors truly complimented the feel of the neighborhood and the feel of our life at the time. On the walls of our condo, I'd hung some of my favorite paintings of flamenco dancers in their beautiful flowing dresses and dramatic poses. I'd been studying flamenco the past few years, and I loved having this theme resonating through our home. *Our home.* That phrase barely meant anything anymore.

My favorite cafe was just across the street and down the block, and it served the most delicious tres leches and cafe con leche I'd ever had. In summers past, it had been a regular stop for us on the weekends on the way home after the walks we'd take in the neighborhood, something we loved doing when the weather was nicer. Now, it was the dead of winter with snow on the ground, heavy winds and gray skies. I didn't mind the cold and brisk air, as it helped calm the nausea of pregnancy, and I felt overheated most of the time carrying this new little life inside me. It was a good time of year to be this pregnant.

My heart ached as I shoved my hopes and dreams into empty boxes. *How had I gotten myself into this situation?* The reality of my life was hardly even fathomable. I found one of Dylan's notebooks on a bookshelf I was emptying and gingerly sat my newly rounded physique down cross-legged on the area rug of our living room, resting the bottom of the notebook atop my expanding belly. I flipped the spiralbound book open. His handwriting was etched on the pages crisply; it was always so neat. I scanned the pages, reading lyrics to songs he had written over the years, including the one he sang to me at our wedding just over five years ago.

At our reception at the Congress Plaza Hotel in downtown Chicago on a beautiful autumn day, he had serenaded me in front of 250 guests, completely surprising me with a song he had written. I was seated across from him in the middle of the ballroom as he strummed along with his guitar, dressed in a cream-colored Spanish style wedding gown, with elegant lace wrapped tightly around my torso and a corset satin tie crisscrossing up my back. I'd worn my long black hair in loose curls draped down my back with just a few wisps framing my face. Handsome in his black tuxedo, Dylan's wedding attire was a strong juxtaposition to his typical jeans, plaid shirts, sneakers, and five o'clock shadow. Singing, he was most at home with himself.

Half Chinese and half Caucasian, with a goatee and small eyes that held a lot of emotion, Dylan was a coffee and cigarettes type of guy. And though he worked as an analyst at a law firm, his persona was much more a match to that of a struggling musician, writing songs into the night and always seeming to be deep in thought. When he had bumped into me at a statistics class at DePaul University years prior, there was an immediate connection. I was an extremely conscientious student who regularly sat in the front row of the classroom, taking careful notes and asking the professor questions to make sure I completely understood the material. Dylan always sat in the back, cracking jokes with a couple of his buddies, but he seemed to grasp all the concepts we were learning with ease. Walking to a lab session one day, we happened to start talking, and his sense of humor won me over. We became good friends and then a couple in a matter of months. On more than one occasion, he told me that he'd dreamt about me before we even met and had visions of us having children. I was flattered at how forward he was, and by the intensity of our relationship when we started dating. He was passionate, and I was at that point in our lives his muse. His lyrics and the way he sang were influenced by his favorite singer Howie Day, who wrote incredibly romantic ballads and had a similar energy to Dylan's.

...It's the way that you make me feel
It's this love, it's something real
It's the look in your eye
It's this love I can't deny
It's this love I can't deny...

We had already danced our first dance as husband and wife, performing a routine that we had practiced for the past four months at the Arthur Murray Dance School downtown. We nailed the Viennese waltz choreography perfectly and laughed as he twirled me around in my dress. I loved how he humored my love of dance and was game to learn a routine like this and perform it in front of so many people. The ballroom was spectacular, appropriately named the "Gold Room," and the Victorian style of the room transported us into another era. After over a year of planning, we'd created a beautiful backdrop to start our new lives together.

The words and the melody of the song running through my memory seemed to stir up the blood running through my body. My heart ached in my chest. Suddenly I felt a cold, wet sensation in my left hand, and I snapped the notebook shut. Our nine-year-old dog, Rolo, a chocolate Labrador mix, was nuzzling up against my hand. He eyed me sadly. Looking into his deep brown eyes, I knew he could feel my pain and wanted to console me.

I shook off the feeling of our wedding day quickly. Though a mere five years had passed, it genuinely seemed like a lifetime ago. I patted Rolo on the head and kissed it. I put my arms around him and was immediately grateful to have somebody to hug. At least *he* still loved me.

Dylan had informed me that he had never loved me just four weeks earlier. Now, after desperately trying to convince him that we should stay together, I had failed. A marriage counselor had worked with us intensely over these past few weeks after our marriage suddenly collapsed, and during a private session with her, I begged her to give me the right answer.

When is enough, enough? Should I have left him already? At what point is it time to file for divorce? And when she told me gently and apologetically that this was a choice that I had to make on my own, I decided for my sanity that it was time to move out. Dylan didn't seem to have an exit strategy beyond telling me he didn't love me, and in the thick fog of his indecision, I decided to let him stay in our condo while I moved back home with my parents, about a 30-minute drive away in the suburbs of Chicago. Where we'd end up after that was still to-be-determined. I had hoped with everything I had that we would work through this and make our family whole before our son was born, but time was ticking, and I had to have a home ready for the baby.

Daggers dug into my heart as Dylan walked right past me while I lifted heavy boxes, not even offering a hand, not even looking me in the eye. He hadn't even acknowledged me before he snapped the door shut to leave for work that morning. What a crazy departure from the loving life we had started together years ago.

A month prior, I had been on top of the world. I was thirty-two, traveling for work, and with an important new client in North Carolina. After two days filled with presentations and meetings, I headed back to the airport in Charlotte to catch my flight home. I was a young professional, a career brimming with promise, stepping outside my comfort zone, but nailing every step perfectly. I was more excited about my profession than ever before, and even through the first four months of pregnancy, I was a road warrior. The fact that Dylan didn't seem very excited about it didn't register for me at the time. I had chalked up all of his latest behavior as him preparing to be a father.

I had tried calling him a few times on the way to the airport, but he wasn't picking up. Dylan had been bad at picking up calls lately.

Shrugging it off, I let my mind wander off to work, pulled out my notebook, and jotted down a quick list of the things I needed to prepare for the client the next day.

While in Charlotte, I had texted Dylan some profile views of my expanding belly, proud of how I was carrying our baby. I let him know that "we" were thinking about him. I was pregnant and so proud, loving the feeling of this baby growing inside me. I wanted to hear the sound of Dylan's voice. I tried calling one more time. He finally answered.

"Hello?" He answered gruffly. It sounded like I had woken him up from a nap. It was seven in the evening.

"Hey, it's me. I've been trying to reach you. Why weren't you picking up? Are you sleeping?" I asked.

"I've been in the gym. I didn't have my phone on me. I told you I've been trying to work out at night." I could tell my phone call had annoyed him.

I said something I had never told him before. "I feel like you're ignoring me. I just wanted to check-in. I've been missing..." He cut me off.

"Like I said, I've been working out. My phone wasn't on me."

"Well, okay. I just wanted to hear your voice. I'll be at O'Hare at 8:45 tonight. Could you pick me up? I'm so exhausted."

He paused. "If you're so tired, can you pick up a cab at the airport? You'll get home faster. I'm tired too." He was probably right; I would get home quicker. I hoped he'd be in a better mood when I got back. I wanted him to feel the baby kicking in my belly. It was happening even more forcefully now, and I didn't want him to miss it.

On the flight home, I worked on some documentation for my customer and let my mind be fully immersed in my work. My new VP, Ali, was behind me and helping to push me to the next stage of my career. With a management background from Accenture, Ali was a force at our company, changing the way our business ran and growing revenue faster than we'd ever seen before. Ali was a tall Pakistani gentleman with a bold taste for fashion and the finer things in life. It was quite common for him to accent his neatly pressed button-down shirts and trousers with a fancy bright-colored designer belt and matching Prada shoes. And while we sometimes joked about his penchant for over the top accessories, he indeed was a genius in his own right, his mind so sharp and his ability to sell so innate that it impressed our CEO and board members profoundly. Somehow, he had chosen me to be one of the closest people he coached. I was fortunate and took his mentorship seriously, throwing myself entirely into the business and learning as I went. Consulting was a newer, but a natural extension of what we offered, and I couldn't have been prouder to be part of a fresh breath of life in our company.

Busily typing into my laptop, I felt a swish in my belly from the amazing little boy or girl that would be entering my life very soon. He or she was moving around quite a bit after having dinner! Things were about to change in a major way, and I was thrilled. Everything seemed to be coming together.

I couldn't wait to tell Dylan about the funny stories of my interactions with Jerry, our very animated sales rep, who was playing the role of consultant to my team at the time. Jerry was a broad-shouldered, middle-aged salesman from New Jersey with black brimmed glasses, a flair for the dramatic, and a sharp tongue. He'd made a small fortune for himself from businesses he'd run in the past and was now branching out and doing consulting work. He was vastly experienced in Product Information Management (PIM) and was one of the thought leaders in tailoring a product in that space towards global data synchronization, which was the niche industry my company was in. When Ali started our consulting division, he'd hired Jerry to work with my team, and it was perfect timing. I was new to the PIM space, and I wanted to squeeze every bit of knowledge out of Jerry that I could. Jerry had a particular affinity for the North Carolina Tarheels and had asked if Dylan and I could catch a game with him at some point since we were in North Carolina so often these days. I thought it was a great idea. Jerry talked about a mile a minute, his mind jumping from one point to the next, always passionate about his opinions. I could see how his scare tactics could easily convince customers to spend money as pre-emptive measures to prevent the disasters he predicted might happen. It made me laugh. I was glad to be making friends in the industry.

The cab pulled up to my building, and I felt relieved. I pulled my suitcase in the front lobby and caught a glimpse of my reflection against the glass doors as I was walking into the elevator. Amazingly, my belly looked bigger than it had at the beginning of the week. On the third floor, the doors opened, and I walked to my front door. Dragging my suitcase in behind me, I'd already started a conversation with Dylan as I walked in. "You wouldn't believe what Jerry pulled off this week…" A couple of sentences in, and I looked over at him, sitting on the couch. The television was off, which was rare since he made it a habit of keeping it on, even for a bit of background noise. It was oddly silent. He looked so serious that it startled me. I knew something was terribly wrong.

My heart stood still for a moment. "What's wrong?" I asked. He just looked at me, some kind of anger bubbling up underneath the surface and, at the same time, looking desperately sad. He didn't say a word. I felt adrenaline rush through my body. I walked over to the couch. I'd seen him upset before, mainly when we fought, but that wasn't very often, and we hadn't even fought recently. This time it felt different.

"What's wrong?" I pleaded again. "Please talk to me. Did something happen at work?" I kneeled on the floor in front of him and put my hands on his lap. I looked up to his face as he sat on the couch. He wouldn't look at me. I was clueless, just trying to start sentences so he'd have somewhere to begin. That was a lot like our entire relationship – I'd give something a start, hoping that he'd jump in and continue. Just like when I'd helped him put together his resume to get started on the job hunt a few years ago. Dylan had had a tough go at corporate life after graduation, and when job openings ran thin post-9/11, he was beyond discouraged. When I could sense him giving up, I intervened by scouring every opportunity I could find online, writing cover letters, and even filling out applications until he landed some interviews.

After another minute, he finally broke the silence.

"I don't love you." His voice shook. "We're just friends. I don't love you. I never loved you."

My heart dropped into my stomach. He started sobbing, pushed me aside, and fell to the floor; his entire body was shaking. Between gasps of air and his sobbing, I heard him say, "I didn't want this for you. I don't love you. I'm sorry." He moaned uncontrollably. I had never seen him like this.

I felt my stomach turn, as our baby shifted around inside me. I looked down at him, utterly confused. I didn't have a chance to react. I was too shocked to feel anything. I felt my hands turn cold, and my heart started pounding. Finally, snapping into action, I put my hand on my stomach and stood up. "Are you telling me I'm about to be a single mother?"

In that instant, I knew my life was never going to be the same. He couldn't respond. The container that held my life, that seemed so neatly tucked, organized, and decorated had broken apart.

Chapter 2: Shell Shocked

I didn't sleep at all that night. I sat wide awake on my side of the bed, my back propped up against some pillows, staring at the ceiling and occasionally looking over at Dylan. He was breathing heavily and peacefully. I was dumbfounded at how he could accomplish that so easily. After his announcement, we had spent all evening talking about what wasn't working in our marriage. I acknowledged that there were obvious holes. Besides my incredibly busy work schedule, I was still doing photoshoots some weekends (I'd picked up photography as a hobby many years prior, and it quickly turned into a lucrative side job that consumed a lot of my time and energy). When Dylan and I would be at home together in the evenings, I spent more time looking at my computer editing photos than I did looking at him. I'd also started working out with a trainer twice a week, so I would leave home at 5 am regularly.

On top of that, I'd joined a book club that met once a month on Saturday nights. It seemed I was addicted to being too busy. Meanwhile, he'd started taking acting classes as his new hobby, and we'd barely spent any quality time together in the past few months. We hadn't adequately addressed where we would end up living with our baby, whether that was the city or the suburbs, and hadn't made the time to sit down and really decide on it as a couple. I was steadfast in my decision that I wanted to work on our marriage. The thought of having a broken family before the baby even arrived was not something I was willing to accept without a fight. He didn't feel the same.

"What did I miss that was so bad?" I pleaded. "Where did I go wrong?"

"Look," he said in an exhausted whisper. "Somewhere along the way, I realized I wasn't attracted to you. I don't know when it happened. I can see that you are pretty, but you're just not for me."

His words, spoken so matter-of-factly, knocked the wind right out of my gut. I looked down at my belly again and felt my sweet baby stirring inside. *After ten years together, now he tells me?* I'd spent the best years of my life building a future with him, and now, at over five months pregnant, I'm just 'not for him'? *God, what do I do now? What could I possibly say to make a difference?* I took a deep breath, holding in every ounce of composure I had left.

"I have no idea how to change your mind about that," I replied, my voice starting to crack with emotion. I felt my heart breaking from the inside out. "All I can tell you is I'm willing to try to save our marriage, for the sake of our baby. Please sleep on it, and let's try our best."

"Fine," he replied unconvinced. "I'm going to sleep."

At about 3 am, a deep fear was steadily working its way through my body. I turned on the lamp at my bedside and looked over at him again. The purple duvet cover was pulled over his head as if he were hiding from me. I could see it rising up and down as he breathed deeply. I'd always loved our gorgeous Calvin Klein duvet with its bamboo floral pattern; it soothed me when I looked at it. We had put it on our wedding registry years ago, and we were so in love with it that we'd also bought a matching set for our second bedroom. *Was this our final night lying in bed together in this beautiful bed? How could he possibly sleep after dropping this news on me?* As badly as I wanted to wake him, I let him be. *You can't force someone to love you.* I rolled myself to the edge of the bed and swung my feet around to pull myself up. It was getting harder and harder to move around the bigger the baby grew. At the foot of our bed, Rolo stirred but did not get up. I patted him softly as I stood up.

I strolled down the unlit hallway and felt my way into the second bedroom. We'd been treating this room more like a storage room these days, so whatever didn't fit in the living room ended up here. My feet knocked right into the boxes lying on the floor as I stumbled in. Still in the dark, I slowly moved to the computer table in the corner of the room, rolled the black leather swivel chair back, and sat down. Moving the mouse around to wake up the computer, the bright screen of my desktop stared back at me blankly. *What am I looking for?* A prayer maybe. A sign from God to tell me what to do next. *Wouldn't it be nice if I could just chat with God online?* He could tell me exactly what to do and what lessons I'd learn, I fantasized.

I'd only had one other life experience with fear this palpable – back in college at Loyola University. As a freshman, I'd felt I'd completely lost my way, realizing I had no idea what classes interested me, what major I would declare, or if I'd even made the right choice in school. That, coupled with the fact that I was in an unhealthy relationship with a new boyfriend who was quick to point out I seemed to be gaining the "freshman fifteen," and was constantly reminding me that I needed to color my hair blonde and have my nails done was enough to rattle my young spirit. All that uncertainty swung wildly around in my head until I'd convinced myself that my life would end up in shambles, and I should just give up. I wasn't used to feeling like a failure. Up until this point in my life, I'd always been a straight-A, happy student.

One day, I had had a full-on panic attack in between classes. That led to the onset of a deep depression less than a week later, which was fear sustaining in my body to the point that I felt my body should no longer exist. I was so lethargic, and I could barely get out of bed; I hardly recognized my face in the mirror. When these feelings lingered on for more than a few weeks, my mother, guided by her deep sense of faith, snapped into action.

Someone at church had told her about a "man of miracles," a healing priest named Fr. Peter Mary Rookey, and suggested we try to attend one of his services. My mother found out where his next service was and convinced me to go. On a cold February afternoon, my mother and I drove to a church in Milwaukee, Wisconsin, where Fr. Rookey was traveling as part of his regular rotation throughout the Midwest. In the car, she and I talked a lot about my depression, and we were both equally perplexed by it. "I don't want to feel this way, mom," I said to her. "I hope this works." Bundled up in her gold-colored winter coat and matching hat, with her makeup done flawlessly, she looked beautiful. Her skin looked as young and healthy as ever. I was glad to have those genes flowing through my blood.

"Let's have faith, darling," she told me as she started recounting stories of healing that she had heard about through her friend. She held her rosary while I drove us. We said some prayers together on the way.

I was not sure what to expect, sitting in the pews of the beautiful basilica that evening. But I opened myself up to the possibility of a miracle. I'd been going to church regularly with my family for my entire life – our Filipino heritage had Catholicism deeply embedded into it, and my faith ran as deep as my parents' did. I looked around at the hundreds of other worshipers, knowing that they, too, needed a miracle and decided at that moment that the miracle was possible for all of us. Fr. Rookey processed in wearing a dark vestment and carrying a black servite rosary in his hand. Something about his aura was undeniably potent, and I immediately leaned forward in my seat and peered at him to get a better look. As he walked up towards the altar, he began to speak, and I noticed that his voice seemed to cut through the air and talk directly to your soul. We prayed the rosary together fervently. This was unlike any church service I had been to before. I prayed with all my heart, clinging to his every word. I no longer wanted sadness to define me.

Fr. Rookey told us that sometimes during his services, people were spontaneously healed. Some people, once blessed with the holy oil during the ceremony, would shake and fall to the ground, fully experiencing the Holy Spirit entering their body. Others would smell the sweet scent of the Holy Spirit and would experience the healing over the next days and weeks. As part of the service, we all lined up to receive a blessing. Fr. Rookey would anoint us with a blessed oil placed on our foreheads in the sign of the cross. I saw people in line ahead of me and, sure enough, some of Fr. Rookey's helpers carefully helped to lay people on the ground so they could safely experience the healing of the Holy Spirit. I saw two people on the ground at the front of the church, peacefully laying with eyes closed, as I walked by. *Wow, is this for real? I'm not ready to fall over in front of all these people!*

When it was finally my turn at the front of the line, Fr. Rookey looked at me and gazed just above my head, saying a prayer and pushed the holy oil into my forehead. I was a bit surprised by the strength of his thumb pressing into my head, and he firmly pushed it again when he said *Amen.* A warm feeling entered my body from head to toe, and as I began to walk away to get back to my seat, I felt my abdomen start trembling. I looked down and could see my body physically shaking. "Hold it together," I told myself, and I concentrated intensely on walking back to my spot in the pew, my mother following closely behind me. I turned around to look at her and whispered sharply, "I'm shaking, are you?"

She shook her head and whispered, "No." My mother looked at me in concern. "Are you okay, baby?" I reassured her I was, and we sat down closely together.

After a few minutes, Fr. Rookey instructed us to pray together again, and I closed my eyes, listening to the almost melodic chanting as we said the Hail Mary in unison. It was beautiful. And with my eyes still closed, suddenly, a fragrant scent entered my awareness; it was sweet and floral and lovelier than anything that I had smelled before. It was powerful and delicate at the same time. It seemed to fade in and out of my awareness, just as the scent of flowers disappear quickly as your face pulls away from a bouquet. It was almost as if this scent was moving around me. My eyes shot open, half expecting there to be a bouquet of roses in front of my face. I looked around the church, and there were no flowers anywhere in my vicinity. But the scent remained and seemed to embrace me. My eyes filled with tears. "Mom, do you smell it?" I asked her.

"Smell what, baby?" she asked me honestly, her eyes still focused on Fr. Rookey at the front of the altar. I realized I was experiencing healing, meant exclusively for me.

"The roses, Mom," I responded as I grabbed her hand. "I smell the fragrance of the Holy Spirit. I'm going to be fine Mama." I squeezed her hand gently and rested my head on her shoulder. *Thank you, God, I feel you. I know I'll be okay.*

And in a couple of weeks, I was. At home the next day, the light started entering back into my eyes. Day by day, I began to feel alive again, and before I knew it, life returned to normal. My spirit had found its way home.

Now, sitting in the dark, I crouched in front of a computer. I was in a cramped bedroom; it was 3 am, and I was over five months pregnant. I prayed for another miracle. *God, please talk to me. Tell me what to do.*

My google chat app opened up automatically as my computer finished waking up, and when it launched, I could see one of my closest friends and colleagues, Cristina, was online.

"Are you there???? Need to talk." I typed in urgently. Cristina had been my best friend at work for the past decade. I'd been to her wedding in New Mexico eight years ago, and she was there for mine in Chicago. We'd shared so much history, both personally and professionally. I wanted her to know what I was going through at this god-awful hour. My heart was racing. I waited anxiously for a reply. After five minutes, I realized it was a false alarm. She wasn't there. I took a deep breath. There'd be no one to chat with or call right now.

I launched the browser and in the search engine, typed in "Marriage Counselors in Chicago." A list of possibilities immediately flooded my screen. "Okay," I thought to myself, "I'm not the only one in Chicago who's been through this. There are professionals to help with these things." This was no time for me or my spirit to collapse. There was so much more on the line this time. I was much more self-sufficient than the nineteen-year-old version of myself that survived that bout of the depression years ago. I needed a miracle and would create one for myself. If there was any shred of hope, I'd latch onto it and do everything I could to help our marriage survive.

Methodically clicking through each link that returned in the search, I saved some contact information and website links that seemed promising, copying and pasting information into an email to myself. I would reach out and talk to people later that day, I decided. I also scanned through articles about marriage counseling, divorces, and life after divorce. I read stories of couples who had somehow saved their marriages and hoped with all my heart that I could be one of them. I checked the time on the corner of my computer screen. 4:16 am. I suddenly felt delirious. I turned off the computer and peeked into the bedroom. Dylan was still sound asleep. Part of me wanted to check his phone, to see who he'd been texting with lately, and to understand if there were any new friends or even new women in his life. But I didn't.

Instead, I walked into our master bathroom to wash my face. I locked eyes with my reflection in the mirror. *Was this really happening?* My face was rounder than I was used to, but so was the rest of me. I was petite in frame, standing at just shy of five feet tall, and before I'd gotten pregnant, I hovered around 115 pounds and worked out regularly. Now, I was closer to 130 pounds, but being as fit as I was, I was carrying the baby weight quite well. Most people could not tell I was pregnant unless they saw my side profile. My hair was cut in a chic short bob that I'd been sporting for the last few years. My eyebrows were still freshly plucked, and my nails perfectly manicured, as I'd made sure I cleaned up well before I'd gotten on the plane to North Carolina. *Pretty. Just not for him. Ugh.* I walked back to our bed and sunk back into it, next to this stranger who was my husband. I shut my eyes.

At 6 am, I rolled out of bed. Dylan was going to be getting up soon, and I had no idea how to interact with him. I got in the shower quickly, bringing my clothes into the bathroom with me, so he wouldn't see me getting dressed. I dried my hair and did my makeup, and though I usually didn't, I put some concealer on under my eyes to try to hide the fact that I'd only slept for an hour. I felt my stomach grumble. The baby was hungry. I had to take care of that. Out of the bathroom, Dylan was standing in our walk-in closet, picking out his clothes for the day. For just a moment, we made eye contact. *Please tell me this wasn't real. You've loved me for ten years. How does it end in one night?* He quickly turned away and headed towards the bathroom.

"I looked up some marriage counselors last night," I mentioned as he walked past me.

"Can we talk about this later?" he replied. He was never a morning person and hated when I'd try to start conversations before he'd adequately waken up for the day. I gave him his space.

"Okay, I'll text you later. Please take Rolo out before you go, I'm heading to the office now." On the way out the door, I grabbed some crackers and a bottle of water from the kitchen. Though I didn't feel much like eating, I knew leaving my stomach empty would be bad for the baby. I forced down a few bites.

On a typical day, I'd stand at the bus stop at the corner of 16th and Halsted and take the #8 bus heading north to Madison, where I'd then walk for a half a mile to the office. Today, I just didn't have the strength to be around a crowd of people. I decided to drive to the office and pay the $35 parking fee in a garage across the street from my office building; I needed that luxury today. Pulling out of my building on Halsted in our green Honda Pilot, I grabbed my phone and found "Charmaine" in my contacts. My sister would be the first person to know what was happening.

"Hey!" I heard on the other end of the line. Charmaine was always upbeat when I called, so full of energy. She was the kind of person who never stood still. She lived near my parents in Glenview, with her husband Lance, their two young children, Valentina and Liam, and her stepson Christian. Charmaine had previously been working in corporate for about eight years before she and her husband Lance decided she should stay home and care for their two young children. However, the "stay-at-home-mom" thing did not slow her down one bit. She signed her children up for every activity they were old enough to participate in. She was a volunteer for her children's school and regularly helped out her parish, St. Catherine's, with every function they had. She was fully engaged in the mom's life and loving every minute of it. Charmaine was my confidant in life, from career to personal life and everything in between. She was a couple of years older than me, and she'd always had an instinct to protect me. "How was your trip?" She remembered me mentioning I'd be in North Carolina this week.

"Are you sitting down?" I asked her seriously.

"Uh, do I need to be? Why do you sound so strange?" She paused. She knew something was terribly off. "Is it the baby?"

"Well, I have some news. Really, please sit down." I paused. I didn't know how to explain this but tried to be as precise as possible. "I think I'm about to be a single mom."

There was silence on the other end of the line for what felt like minutes.

"Are you serious? What does this mean? What the hell happened?" I could hear some anger rising in her voice.

"Well, I got home from Charlotte last night, and as soon as I walked in the door, Dylan told me he didn't love me anymore. I think I'm in shock. I wasn't expecting this at all. I mean, we've been looking for a house, and I... God, I don't know Char." I recounted what had happened over the past evening. I told her I'd convinced him we needed to try counseling.

"Vaness, listen," she interjected. She sounded like she'd made her own conclusion. "You have always been a rising star, and I don't think he can handle it. I think he's jealous of your success." Truth be told, my marriage to Dylan had been a point of contention for her. She had warned me in the past that she felt like a part of him still needed to grow up, and she wanted to make sure I was taken care of. I'd brushed her opinion aside and assured her that we were both committed and had a partnership that worked for us. I'd always believed that. So, for me, she had put her opinions aside, and we'd carried on with our lives.

"You think so? Maybe you're right. I don't know. I'm about to have his baby, and I think I need to fight to save my marriage."

"I know, I'm so sorry," she softened her tone. "You're right to feel that way. Maybe he will snap out of this. Maybe it's cold feet about being a father. Do you have to be at work all day? Let's meet up," she suggested. "Just come home." By home, she meant my parent's house in Morton Grove.

I pulled into the parking lot in the building across the street from work and sat there. I was still too shell shocked to cry. The thought of seeing Charmaine at my parents' house tonight sounded comforting. Her steady reassurance gave me a tiny shred of hope that I could handle whatever was about to come.

Chapter 3:
The Day the Music Stopped

At work that morning, I poured my heart out to my boss, Tammy, who was also a trusted friend. Tammy had been my manager for the past several years, and she had always given me good perspective. I'd asked her to meet me in the large conference room in the corner of our office with a view overlooking the Chicago River and the Lyric Opera House. With large windows surrounding the corner of the office, the morning light illuminated the room with a soft glow. Sitting across from her, I saw the look on her face shift from curiosity to deep concern as I relayed my current situation. "I'm in uncharted territory," I explained. "I'm scared beyond belief."

Tammy's long platinum blonde hair always fell perfectly into place, and with a black and white checkered scarf wrapped around her neck and draped over her shoulders, she looked sophisticated and polished. Her eyes were the kind that seemed to pierce right into you, informing you that she was really listening. "Vanessa, I am completely shocked," she said honestly. "I've always admired your relationship with Dylan. He's always seemed so dedicated and so *into* you. I thought you two were so happy together. I'm confused about this too. I just never would have imagined… I'm so sorry…" I could see she wanted to help. "You don't have to be at work today, but I completely understand if you want to be here too." She understood how I operated. I needed to be in my typical environment today to get by.

"Thank you so much for your support," I responded. "I want to be here today. I have a couple of client calls to handle, but if it's okay with you, I'll probably hide out in one of our phone booth rooms to try to find a marriage counselor too."

She stood up and walked around the table to give me a reassuring hug. "Anything you need," she said. I was grateful for her compassion, and the mere fact that she knew seemed to fuel me with enough strength to get through the next few hours. I headed down towards the other end of the office and decided I'd park myself there for the rest of the day. I felt my phone buzz with a new text message. It was my mother-in-law, Karol. Earlier that morning, I had texted her, asking her to talk. My message had been rather casual as I did not want to alarm her. In the ten years we had known each other, I had never reached out to her to talk one-on-one before, but I needed all the support I could get. I thought somehow, she might be able to help me turn this around. She had given birth to Dylan at the young age of 19 when she'd met and married her first husband. When Dylan was less than two years old, her husband had walked out on them. Dylan told me how much he ended up appreciating his stepfather, Dan, whom Karol had met a few years later, and how Dan felt like his real father. Later in life, Dylan had made amends with his biological father and invited him to our wedding. He was a distant family member, but still, one that Dylan accepted fondly. I wondered to myself if history was going to repeat itself.

My phone dinged with Karol's response: *Hi there! You bet. I'll be available at noon your time if you want to give me a call.*

I responded right back:
That's perfect. I'll give you a call then. Thanks!

I tried to wrap my head around what to say to her as I started working through the list of marriage counselors I'd found. My heart raced. I needed someone good, right now. The first four prospects I called went straight to voicemail. I left messages and continued. On the fifth call, a man with a gentle voice picked up the phone. *Finally! I need to talk to a real person.* He was the owner of the therapy practice, as he explained, and while his secretary was out, he was answering all calls. *Thank God.* I thought to myself. *An expert is on the line.*

"How can I help you, Vanessa?" he said genuinely. For the third time this morning, I explained what was going on. "With our baby almost here, I need to sort this out ASAP," I implored. I wanted this stranger to tell me he could fix this.

"I am so sorry that you are going through this," he said. "As confusing a time as this is, regardless of whether you stay together or not, what is most important is this: How do both of you live lives that you can be happy with?" That is what we aim to help you figure out. You can both live happy lives, no matter how this turns out." The thought of living my life without Dylan by my side and being happy about it was anathema to me, but any step forward at this point seemed like progress. The owner set me up with an appointment with one of his therapists named Meg, who would meet with us at our condo in a few days. He emailed me some intake forms to fill out. I printed them off immediately, filled out as much information as I could, and put them in my backpack. I texted Dylan and asked him if he could meet me at Starbucks at 2 pm to finish the paperwork.

"I'll be there," he responded.

It was almost noon. I dialed my mother-in-law's number and took a deep breath. "Hello?" I heard on the other end of the line. She sounded upbeat, likely waiting for me to ask for baby advice, I imagined.

"Hi, Mom," I said, sounding like I was on the verge of tears.

"What's wrong, sweetie?" she said. Karol was an executive at a pharmaceutical company in Indianapolis. She had always been so welcoming of me into their family, and she was over the moon when she found out that she was going to be a grandmother. I thanked her for taking the time out to talk to me in the middle of her busy day.

"I don't know how to say this…" my voice trailed off. I was tired of relaying the story, but I needed her to know. "I got home from a business trip last night, and when I arrived, Dylan told me he didn't love me and never had. We spent the whole night talking, and I don't know if I can change his mind. I'm in shock, and I'm trying to figure this out. I found a marriage counselor this morning. I'm trying to make this work…"

"Oh, Vanessa…" I could hear the devastation in her voice. There was silence for a minute while she composed herself. "I know he loves you. This isn't right. I always thought having a therapist might be good for him." She started reminiscing about some of the troubles Dylan had had when he was a teenager. "I have to believe he's getting cold feet about being a father. You did the right thing in finding a counselor. *Please* don't give up."

"I won't." I responded. "I just can't control all of this… I don't know what will happen next, Mom. What if he doesn't come around?" Karol said she would talk to Dan, and they'd give Dylan a call tonight. She promised we would talk again soon.

At a quarter to 2 pm, I walked down to the Starbucks that was halfway between Dylan's office and mine. Over the years, we'd made a habit of meeting there after work so we could have some coffee and walk home together in the evenings. I sat at our usual spot with the paperwork spread out on the table. There was a section for me to fill out and a section for him. I read through mine.

Last night my husband told me he has never loved me. I was not expecting this at all and believed we had a good relationship up until this point. I am five and a half months pregnant, and I want to do everything I can to save our marriage.

I thought about things I could have done better, like being more present when we did have time together in the evenings. I sorely regretted being overbooked with work, grad school, and my photography business over the past few years. I must have lost him somewhere along the way. A desperate side of me now wanted this to all go away, and for Dylan and I to continue living our lives, pretending yesterday had never happened. We'd go to the movies this weekend like we usually did, share a large popcorn and a blue raspberry Icee and have some mini-burgers at PJ Clarke's afterward.

"Hey," I heard and looked up to see Dylan making his way towards me. He grabbed a seat across the table from me, which was unlike the Dylan I knew. *That* Dylan always chose the seat right next to me. He looked tired.

"Hi," I said and tried to smile. "I found a therapist today. Her name is Meg, and I think she's going to be really good. I filled in everything I could, and there's just one section I need you to fill out here." I pointed to the blank lines on the form. He pulled a pen out of his backpack and didn't say a word. He scribbled a few lines in quickly, and I tried not to look like I was hovering. He stacked the papers back together again and handed me the pile. "Are you doing okay today?" I said as I shoved the papers into my backpack.

"Not really," he wouldn't look at me.

"I'm going to my parent's house tonight."

"That's fine." His body language told me everything I needed to know. He didn't want to be near me at all. I felt the bond I thought we once had slipping right through my fingers and wished I had just the right words to say to convince him this was something we could fix. As sleep-deprived as I was, there was so much fear worked up in me that I couldn't feel the exhaustion.

I put my hand over his across the table. "I still want to work this out," I said with as much confidence as I could muster. I looked at his face until his eyes met mine. Almost immediately, he pulled his hand back and stood, picking up his backpack and putting the straps on his shoulders.

"I have to get back to work." Without any kind of acknowledgement of what I'd just said, he turned around and walked away.

As I watched him walk out the door, I scanned the room, my face hot with embarrassment. *Did anyone notice?* Starbucks was bustling with people, yet no one had seen what had just transpired. No, it was just me sitting here with my shame and disappointment and no one to share it with me but the baby in my womb. *I'm sorry, baby. I'll do my best to make this right for you.*

My stomach grumbled, and I shook off my daze of disappointment. I ordered a spinach wrap and a bottle of Pellegrino and sat down to eat by myself. As I sat there, I slid the stack of papers out of my backpack and read the comments he had written into our intake form:

I have lost all my feelings for my wife. I would like to sort out the next steps.

That was it. Tears started to form in the corners of my eyes, but I willed them to stop. I refused to break down in front of strangers at a Starbucks. I took a deep breath and headed towards work and back to my car. I couldn't stay for the rest of the day.

On the drive back to the condo, my phone rang. It was Ali.

"Hey," I answered, trying to sound upbeat.

"Vanessa, I got a call from Tammy," he said. I paused, unsure of what I could say next. Tammy, Ali, and I often referred to each other as 'work family,' as we shared personal information quite comfortably, so I was not surprised to be getting this call. And I was relieved to not have to explain it all to him. "Look," he continued. "I want you to know you have my support. What matters most is that you and your baby are okay. I have a lot of faith and hope for you." Tears started streaming down my face, and I wiped them away.

"Thanks, Ali," I responded. "I appreciate it more than you know." I pulled up to my condo and decided to park in front since it would be a quick stop inside.

I packed a duffle bag of clothes and toiletries and took Rolo out for a quick walk. I'd leave him with Dylan for the evening while I went to see my parents and sister. In a matter of twenty minutes, I was back in the car again and headed to Morton Grove. Turning the radio on for the first time today, I was surprised to hear Gwen Stefani's' voice singing, "…I really feel that I'm losin' my best friend… I can't believe this could be the end…." *God, this feels like some kind of sick joke,* I thought to myself. Immediately, I turned the radio off and vowed that I would stop listening to music until I got through this period of my life. The last thing that I wanted was a soundtrack to my heartbreak.

I sat in silence as I turned onto Roosevelt and approached the ramp to I-94, heading north. The 30-minute drive was familiar and comforting. I'd be talking to my mom again in no time, and I'd have the love of my family surrounding me like a warm blanket. I prayed out loud, first an "Our Father," then a "Hail Mary" which I hadn't done in a really long time. But it was my instinct to pray whenever times got difficult.

My parents had been strong pillars in the Catholic community at our local church, St. Martha's in Morton Grove, for decades. My father, David, was a neurologist, and he and my mother, Rosario, moved their lives from the Philippines to the US in the 1970s to test their luck on the promise of a better life in 'the States' as they called it. They had met in medical school at the University of Santo Tomas, a Roman Catholic research university based in Manila. They fell in love and started a family shortly thereafter. Once they decided to move the States, they agreed that my father would go first to get an apartment and get things ready for the family.

My mother joined him six months after and brought along my older brother David, who was just two and a half years old at the time.

Sadly, she left my older sister, six-month-old Charmaine, behind, as she was not able to take both little children along with her for the long journey to America. My grandmother, 'Mommy Titang' as we lovingly called her, would watch over baby Charmaine before finally uniting her with our family a year later.

My father was completing his residency at the University of Louisville in Kentucky when I was born in March of 1979. Not having the help of any family around, my mother agreed to give up her aspirations of a medical career to raise the children, which kept her plenty busy. Surviving on my father's small salary as an intern was a challenge, never mind the cultural shock. Back home in Manila, she had had many luxuries, including a midwife (similar to a nanny in the States). She also had a driver to get her from one place to the next, as well as her parents for moral support. This was a stark contrast to having no support system in the US while my father worked all day and none of the comforts of her homeland. She learned how to cook, how to clean for herself and the kids, and how to live in this new society.

Once, taking the family out to the store after church, as my mother pushed me around in my stroller, dressed in my Sunday best, a man approached my father, calling him a "China Man," mocking him. His intimidating gestures and condescending tone didn't faze my father, who looked him dead in the eye and said, "Sir, I am Filipino," without the slightest hint of an accent. My parents had always spoken perfect English and had studied it long before they ever set sights on living in the States. Our family walked out of the store with heads held high that day. On the drive home, Dad told us, "Never be afraid to speak up for yourself. Let that be a lesson to us all." That was the kind of person my dad was — always confident and sure of himself.

Another time when my mother took us out to the grocery store without my father, a group of white women were clearly amused by the look of my Asian mother toting her three Asian children around. One of them boldly approached us with hands in a prayer pose and bowed deeply at the waist, mocking the Japanese word *Arigato,* before erupting in laughter at my family's expense. Those things were not an everyday occurrence, but they were very real. We never let it steal our joy. Every night, David, Charmaine, and I counted our blessings as we did our evening prayers with Mom. We prayed for God to bless everyone we knew, including those who didn't know better than to treat us differently. It would be many years before I realized how much of a struggle it was for my mom during her transition to life in the States. She never made it an issue for us and protected us from any regrets she had. I grew up happy and extremely loved. She was an amazing mother.

By the time I was three years old, my father had found work in the Chicagoland area and moved our family to Morton Grove, a Northwest suburb, where we rented a small house on Mango Street. Here, we were lucky to find a Filipino community had taken hold, and at St. Martha's, where I would later go to school, I had many Filipino classmates. Over the years, Dad's medical practice thrived, and he was able to build us a brand new, custom-built home in the same town. Our financial status had clearly changed, and he was prouder than ever to be building this dream home for us. This would be the place I remembered as my real home.

My phone rang again. This time it was my dad.

"Hi Daddy," I answered, my voice made thick with tears.

"Hi, baby," he responded softly. "Your mom told me what happened. I'm here for you, anak." *Anak* means *my child* in

Tagalog, the Filipino dialect my parents spoke. "I will take care of this baby with you. I will be a father figure for him, don't worry." My father was always so strong and stoic, but hearing the pain in his voice was enough to move me to tears. "Are you coming home?"

"I'm on the way there, Daddy," I said and broke into more tears. "I'm so scared, Dad." I was his youngest daughter and had always been daddy's little girl. I was immensely relieved to hear how supportive he was, as I'd wondered how he would react to my news. The mere idea of the breakup of my marriage felt like a gigantic failure, and I didn't want to let my dad down.

I had exited the highway and was almost home, driving down a winding street next to the Chick Evans Golf Course in Morton Grove. At about a block away, I could see our house from the road and breathed a sigh of relief. It was a beautiful Spanish style home built in the mid-'80s with a coral-colored brick and arches used to accent the windows, walkway, and garage doors. There was a beautiful wrought iron gate in front of the walkway up to the house, and a red and black roof with a skylight peeking out of one part, making way for natural light to flow into my parents' master bath. Three lantern style light fixtures framed the gate and garage doors, and two trees that my father had planted in front of our house when we were children had grown into lovely accents that framed the left side of the house, providing shade to our front lawn. Our home.

My mom heard me opening the front door and came to meet me as I was walking in. "Hi, baby. I've been so worried about you, mahal." *Mahal* meant *love*. My mom was dressed in a light blouse and cardigan, and dark leggings, looking elegant. Her makeup was perfectly done, her long black hair was pulled back into a loose ponytail, and her fine-wire rimmed glasses were on. Her frame was petite – over the past few years, she'd lost about twenty pounds after finding out she had diabetes. She'd made a quick turnaround in changing her eating habits, stabilizing her health.

I put my bags down on the dark brown tiled floor and put my boots on the oriental style foyer rug. In the foyer area, there was a long marble table, with various religious statues and prayer pamphlets that my mother had collected. Above us was a vaulted ceiling from which hung a large, delicate chandelier that my mother had chosen when we had built the house. With a large open window high above us facing east and overlooking the walkway, when the early morning daylight streamed in, it created little rainbows all around the house as the light passed through the crystals of the chandelier. An acrylic painting of a paper boat floating in a pond of water lilies that my mother had created when I was a little girl, reminiscent of a Monet, was hung with an ornate gold frame next to the front door. Within the painting, she had stenciled the words to the poem "Children Learn What They Live," a homage to the way she viewed her vocation in life in raising her children. "Hi, Mama," I said and gave her a big hug.

"Have you eaten? You have to make sure the baby is okay," she urged as she pulled me towards the kitchen.

I sat down on a stool next to the kitchen island, and my mom served me a cup of hot chamomile tea in a large mug and a piece of Hawaiian bread with strawberry cream cheese on a white plate with pink trim. "Do you want me to heat the Sinigang?" she asked. Sinigang was a traditional Filipino sour soup that my mom made with pork ribs. It was one of my favorite dishes. Without missing a beat, she turned on the stovetop where a large soup pot was already sitting. Chestnut cabinets lined the light green walls, and the U-shaped island encircled my mother as she seamlessly pulled open drawers and cabinets. Sitting on the stool, I felt like she was on stage, and I was watching her production, making snacks and putting away dishes, and chattering mindlessly about what she'd been doing today. It was a nice distraction, and for a moment, I tried to forget about everything else. The baby was moving around in my belly, enjoying our snack. "I'm sorry I've made such a mess," I interrupted, partially talking to my mom, but also talking to my baby.

"There's no mess," my mom said quizzically, looking at the food on my plate.

"I mean the mess I've made of my life," I clarified, with tears starting to sting my eyes again. "I don't know what just happened, but I'm pretty sure I'm about to be a single mom."

"My God, don't apologize," she said sternly. "How could you have known this was going to happen? I've been thinking, anak, his father left him when he was a baby, maybe he didn't feel loved enough as a little boy…" It was sweet of her to try to make sense of it for me, in a way that still viewed him with kindness.

"I always thought he was happy as a kid, Mom. Karol took good care of him even though she worked a lot, and he had Dan as his father. He was fortunate, I think… To be honest, I'm sure I haven't been the greatest wife," I confessed to her. "I've been so focused on my work and traveling that I haven't been able to keep up with normal household duties." It was true. I often lived out of a suitcase and couldn't keep up with the mail, the laundry, or grocery shopping. That left him with a lot of the burden, and I probably didn't seem very grateful. "Maybe I was too busy to see things straight and couldn't even tell he was falling out of love with me."

I heard the front door open. "Vaness?" It was my sister.

"We're in the kitchen," I yelled over to her.

"Okay, I'm coming!" I heard the soft thud of her shoes being kicked off, and then Charmaine was standing at the end of the island facing my mom and me. She'd loosely tied up half of her long black hair in a bun, letting the rest of it fall halfway down her back. She was slender, like my mom, and had a mole just to the right of her nose, in exactly the same spot as my mom, which I always envied as a kid. They looked so similar. Her skin was bare of any makeup minus her eyeliner, which she had always worn religiously. "Vaness, I'm so sorry," she said as she leaned over my chair and threw her arms around me. "We are going to figure this out together."

"Thanks Char." I hugged her back tightly.

"So... what the hell?" she said with an annoyed look on her face. She was never the type to beat around the bush. She fidgeted around at the end of the counter, standing between our mother and me. "He just can't seem to man up when life requires it."

I appreciated her fighting spirit. I didn't respond, knowing she'd fill in the silence with more of what I needed to hear.

"Look, Vaness, like I said earlier, you are a rising star. You don't see it now, but maybe this is the best gift ever."

"I hear you, Char, thank you. I don't know what to say. I know I haven't been the perfect partner either. I honestly feel like an idiot for not knowing he didn't love me."

"Oh, Vaness..." she softened. "I thought he was crazy about you. Maybe he still is. But he has pissed me off, and you just deserve better than this!"

"I just have to do what's right for the baby. I feel like our baby deserves a shot at having us together as a family. I don't want to rob the baby of that. It's just not right."

Her cell phone rang, and she looked up at me. "It's David," she said, referring to our older brother. "I told him what happened." She answered the phone and started chatting with him, pacing back and forth between the kitchen and dining room, giving him the latest updates. I stopped listening after a minute or so and focused on the Sinigang that my mom had placed in front of me, took a heaping spoonful of the steaming white rice she also set out, and placed it right into the soup, enjoying the savory, sour flavor that I'd loved since I was a little girl.

Charmaine handed me her cell phone. "Hey, Dave," I said quietly. My big brother was at least twice as protective of me than Charmaine was, and I was curious to hear what he'd say. I was really close with my brother, especially after having lived with him in college. David was never one to be pushed around. Even though he was a short Filipino guy, he knew how to handle himself in tough situations thanks to his training in Muay Thai kickboxing. I spent my college years hanging out with him and his friends and eventually was there to witness him finding his wife, Ewa, while he was in medical school. He'd become a primary care physician and they had four beautiful children together.

"Vaness… Char looped me into everything that was happening," he said calmly. "I've prayed a couple of rosaries for you today."

"Thanks, bro," I responded. David was so devout and steadfast in his faith; I was sure his prayers went straight to St. Michael the archangel himself. "I'm so shocked and embarrassed. I'm just sitting here trying to figure out what to do next with mom and Char. It's a mess..."

"I know, little sister," he said sweetly. "I'm sorry I am not there with you in person. The kids have me so tied up. You know I'd be there otherwise."

"Oh, Dave, no worries at all. You live so far away," I reminded him. He was living in Tinley Park, over an hour away. The times we had together were becoming fewer and farther between.

"Honestly," he continued, "I'm also praying for God to give me the restraint to not kill him with my own bare hands. If these were different times, he would no longer exist." I chuckled a bit. That was my brother's well-known temper at work. I was glad to have such a strong support system. Suddenly, I heard a child crying in the background.

"Oh, shit, my kid just hit his head," he explained quickly. "I gotta go, Vaness."

"No worries, Dave, take care of him. Talk soon. I love you."

"Love you too, little sis." And we hung up.

"Well, that went well," I joked with my sister. "I think he's gonna kill Dylan."

She put her arm around me and noticed my bowl of Sinigang. "Mom, I'm starving, can I have some of that?"

She sat down next to me and started to fix herself an identical bowl of soup. "Well, what now?" she asked. She paused and gave me a big hug. I could smell the sweet scent of shampoo in her hair as I held onto her longer than I ever had before. I longed to be as strong as she was.

"Is it okay if I borrow some of your strength in the next few months? I'm really going to need it." The pain on her face was palpable. We agreed that I should give marriage counseling a real shot, but that if it didn't work out, I should move back to Morton Grove. Charmaine was only 10 minutes away in Glenview. I was so relieved to know my sister would be with me every step of the way.

Before I knew it, I looked at the clock, and it was after 8 pm. My eyes were weary, and I was fading quickly after having lived what felt like the longest day of my life. Charmaine helped me with my bags to her old bedroom on the second floor. My mom had prepped it with fresh linens and a new comforter before I arrived. I got dressed for bed, and Char gave me one last hug before she went home to her family. As a dutiful older sister, she made sure I was tucked safely into bed as I shut my eyes. Finally, tears started flowing, a fountain of sadness unleashing that I could no longer keep at bay. I put one hand on my belly, and my sister grabbed the other hand. We both cried silently, praying for strength.

Chapter 4: Dusty Road

My dream was vivid as I fell into a deep sleep that night. I was walking down a dusty, winding road in Santa Fe, feeling hot in the mid-day sun, with a bright blue sky ahead and barely any cloud cover in sight. Dark green shrubs were interspersed across the miles that seemed to go on forever. I squinted into the trek I had ahead of me, feeling unsure. I didn't know my destination, but I knew it would be a long journey. I looked back over my right shoulder and saw the building that I'd just left – a peach-colored adobe structure that had been my classroom. It was a place for which I felt so much love. But I'd outgrown it. It felt like a school that I'd been to many times, a familiar training ground. I heard the sound of an engine and looked over my left shoulder.

Seemingly out of nowhere, an old blue Ford pickup truck was approaching, and a middle-aged Native American man waved me over. I knew him. His name was Angel; I'd met him in my dreams before. Without hesitation, I walked over to him and greeted him. His long, wavy, jet black hair hung loosely to his shoulders and framed his face. There were deep wrinkles in his forehead and cheeks, a product of living in the sun for so long. He wore what appeared to be a beige-colored robe, tan-colored trousers, and brown leather sandals. His aura illuminated pure wisdom, seeming to have lived many lives, and having a deep understanding of the universe. He had a big, comforting smile as our eyes met and didn't require any words to communicate with me. He was here to give me a lift. He had one condition - that I would be behind the wheel.

I would be the navigator. I was confused. *But I don't know where to go.* I tried to tell him without words. He smiled and climbed into the back seat.

Trusting he knew what he was doing, I climbed into the driver's seat. Suddenly, I noticed a passenger in the front with me. I couldn't mistake her, with her dark, curly brown hair, high cheekbones, eastern European features, and a sunny smile lined with a beautiful deep pink lipstick. She was wearing a turquoise-colored dress with gold details. Her name was Sonia Choquette. Sonia was a world-renowned best-selling author and spiritual teacher whose work I'd studied for the past several years. She had grown up Catholic and had made many references to it in her books. Her view on spirituality complemented my own beliefs, as well as introduced me to new concepts that helped me navigate the world with more confidence. Namely, that we all had guides and angels around us at all times, waiting for us to tap into their support. *Wow, Sonia, you're here! What are you doing here?* I asked without speaking a word. She gave me a knowing nod and a wink that seemed to say; we're *on our way.*

I drove the truck down that winding road for what felt like hours. It was a feeling of being utterly lost, but in the presence of the most comforting support I could have hoped for. The bright blue sky eventually turned into a deep purplish-pink as the sun set, and finally into an indigo midnight sky with a million beautiful stars lighting the way. I felt Angel urging me forward. *Keep going.*

Chapter 5: Undoing

The following weeks were a blur of activity as the construct of my life changed. I was living out of a suitcase, spending some nights in Morton Grove, and some nights at the Pilsen condo. Each day that passed, I felt Dylan slipping further and further away. Doing my best to keep up with household duties, I prepared meals for us, tidied up around our condo, and tried to be as cheerful as I could. He rarely made eye contact with me, and when we did speak, it was only about what plans he had with classmates from his acting school, and reasons why he wouldn't be home. When he was at home with me, he spent a lot of time sitting out on the balcony by himself, smoking cigarettes. On one such occasion, I opened the sliding glass door and joined him.

"Hey there…" I said carefully. "I was wondering if you'd mind coming with me to the store? I wanted to make some pork chops tonight, and we're out of ginger ale and a few other things I'm craving. I could really use a hand if that's okay." I thought doing normal life activities might bring us closer together again.

Dylan, still gazing out across the street, took a long drag off of his cigarette. Watching the side of his profile, I saw a big puff of smoke go into the air and out towards the street. His clothes looked looser than I remembered. He had lost a lot of weight. As he flicked his cigarette down into the empty gravel parking lot below us, he shrugged his shoulders. "Sure, I'll go with you."

His stepfather, Dan, called him while we were in the produce aisle, and I could tell by the sound of it that Dan was asking him pointed questions. Dylan's face became hot and red, and the pace of his breathing quickened. "Dad, I really need to focus on myself right now…No, I am not afraid of being a father!" He shot back, looking impatient as his eyes darted around the store like a trapped animal.

I slowed my pace, took a breath, and tried to focus on finding the saltines, spaghetti sauce, and apples I was craving. The crowded store and bright aisles full of food gave me something else to focus on besides my heartbreak. Dylan was following closely behind me as he ended his call. That he only wanted to focus on himself right now made my heart sink, but I was trying to be as open-minded as possible. Looking down at my growing belly, I silently prayed. *We really need him to come around soon, God. Please help us.* Pushing the shopping cart down the aisle, I tried not to falter. I looked at Dylan and reminded him, "Hey, we are meeting with Meg tomorrow. She can help us figure all this out." I tried to sound as mellow as possible. My in-laws had called me a couple of times over the past few days, imploring me not to give up and supporting our decision to try counseling. I clung desperately to the idea that our therapist would open his heart up, have a look, and tell me exactly how to fix it.

Before our first session the following evening, I sat at the edge of my seat on the couch, my feet fidgeting, anxiously awaiting her arrival. Dylan waited in our bedroom, keeping as much distance from me as possible.

Our landline rang as Meg dialed us from the call box from downstairs, and I jumped up to buzz her in. I yelled out to Dylan that Meg was here and answered the door as she arrived. Meg was in her early thirties, tall, slender, and red-headed. She wore a beige pea coat, a casual beige sweater and jeans, and a grey cross-body bag with silver zippers. I walked her over to the couch where Dylan now sat. He'd chosen the short end of the L-shaped couch. Meg sat on the other end, and I perched next to Meg in between them. She pulled out a notebook and pen from her bag and then made eye contact with each of us, seeming to indicate our session was about to begin.

"Thank you both for opening yourselves up to me today. I want you to understand my approach and how I work with people. Unfortunately, couples often reach out to a therapist after things have already imploded. An ideal scenario would have been having sessions before that happened, but in this case, it sounds like we're already past that point. That's okay. We can still make progress. We can still figure out healthy ways to move through this painful time. This is a good first step. Tonight, I'll be asking you some questions that you can answer together, and I'll also be asking questions to each of you individually. I'll ask that you respect the other person and allow them to finish their answer before stepping in."

A wave of relief swept over me as I heard the compassion in her tone. I trusted her immediately. Dylan seemed to be engaged as well, as I noticed him leaning forward and listening intently. We spent most of the hour explaining our history together, about how we'd met, and how our relationship had been over the past year. Dylan interjected, "I don't know how to explain it, but I feel like I've been a robot for years, with no real feelings. I just finally realized that I don't love her."

Meg saw the hurt in my face but remained neutral and objective. "We are not going to make any decisions tonight," she announced. "What's clear to me is that Dylan has some work to do on addressing and processing his emotions. I'd like to schedule a session with him separately to get started. Dylan, are you okay with this?"

"Yeah," he shrugged, looking flustered. "I'll give it a try."

"Good. I'd also like you, Dylan, to get a journal to start writing your feelings, and for you to write in it daily. I also think you need to change up your routine to make sure you're doing something for yourself – maybe that means going to the record store for a couple of hours to browse, or watching a band perform... the idea is to do one thing for a couple of hours that is just for yourself, over the next week. Does that sound do-able? We'll continue doing the couple's sessions, of course, so let's plan to do that once a week. Could this be our regular time slot?"

"Yes," I responded without hesitation. I liked her plan. The sting of him confirming his lack of love for me still hurt like hell, but I tried to be hopeful. Though her advice about writing in a journal was intended for Dylan, I clung to the idea and decided I'd do the same.

We ate our dinner of rotisserie chicken and rice that night separately – me standing at the kitchen countertop, and him sitting at his spot on the couch. We were still close enough in proximity to make casual conversation. "I'm done thinking about all this tonight. Do you want to watch a movie or something?" I asked, hopeful that we could spend time bonding over something a little more lighthearted. Dylan scrolled through some options on the TV and landed on a movie we'd never watched, called *Money Ball,* a baseball movie starring Brad Pitt. Thankful to have something else to occupy our attention (especially if Brad Pitt was involved), I laid on the opposite end of the couch with a pillow from our bedroom, wishing that Dylan would snuggle up with me, but knowing he wouldn't. Having no one to hold me while I was pregnant made me feel insecure and lonely. Instinctively, I cradled my belly in my hands and spoke to the baby silently. *I'll always be here to hold you.*

I lost myself in the movie, intrigued by Billy Beane (Brad Pitt) and his brilliant plan to change the way major league baseball fundamentally formulated success. More so, I was moved by how they developed Brad Pitt's character in the movie as a single dad and had highlighted his relationship with his daughter. He seemed to love her intensely but wasn't around for her every day. His daughter lived primarily with her mother, who was happily married to a very well-to-do man. A pang of sadness ran through my body, starting from my chest down, wondering if that was our fate as well. I tried to comprehend how that family had gotten through the sadness of their separation and moved onto happiness at some point. It was a scenario as old as time, of a marriage broken, but I didn't want to be another statistic.

As the movie ended, Dylan announced that he needed to go out to buy cigarettes. While he was gone, I took Rolo for a long walk. We headed north on Halsted and then turned left on 16th, walking along the sidewalk and the thin path of grass and trees that ran alongside the elevated train tracks above us. The concrete walls leading up to the train tracks had some areas that were completely blank, and other areas decoratively painted by local artists. Rolo tugged me along as he liked to keep a quicker pace than I was used to. About half a mile down, I admired the newly developed condo building that Dylan and I had considered originally. It oozed of the artistic vibe of the neighborhood, but the location was just a bit farther west than we wanted to be.

What would our lives have been like if we'd chosen that place instead? Would we have stayed together happily? Would our dynamic have been different in this home? I imagined us making dinner in this alternative life, laughing, and having friends over and being truly happy.

Rolo tugged at me again, ready to move on, and I fell out of my trance. I noticed my hands were freezing. It was pretty late. We turned around and headed home.

Making our way out of the elevator and back into our condo, all the lights were out except the light in the hallway leading to the bedroom. Dylan had hung his jacket on the back of one of the chairs near the front door, and I heard light music playing in the living room. I found Dylan asleep on the couch, with a blanket over him. It looked like he intended to be on the couch for the night. *I guess he won't be sleeping next to me anymore.*

I got ready for bed, and Rolo followed me into the bedroom. He'd keep me company, and I was grateful for that. I let him jump up on the bed to lay with me. Before I fell asleep, a nagging question entered my mind that my family and friends had asked me about: *What if there was another woman?* After about 30 minutes of tossing and turning, I got up and went back towards the living room. With Dylan still asleep, I walked over to his jacket and checked his pockets. I found a fresh pack of cigarettes in one pocket, along with a few crumpled-up receipts, and in the other pocket, I found a business card and a piece of candy in a plastic bag. I used my phone as a light to read the business card. It was a woman named Jessica who worked at a flower shop. I'd heard her name before. She was a classmate from his acting class who I'd seen perform on stage a couple of months ago. I looked at the piece of pink candy in his pocket that was in a plastic bag. It looked like a homemade jolly rancher. I almost ate it on the spot but stopped myself at the last second. I had never before snooped on my husband like this. I felt guilty. I was nervous he'd wake up, angry that I was going through his things. The last thing I wanted was a fight. I figured Jessica had made some candy for some of the class. Dylan was quite fond of his circle of friends at acting school, and this all seemed harmless enough. Shaking my head at my own antics, I put everything back in his pockets and went to bed.

A few days later, we had my 20-week appointment at the doctor. We found out the sex of the baby – a boy! I cried tears of joy when I heard the news from the technician. I looked over at Dylan from my spot on the examination table, hoping to see the same spark of joy. No such miracle occurred. "What a great time for him to have an existential crisis," my doctor later told me in private, rolling her eyes. There was no shortage of words of support from Dr. MacCabe. In her many years of being an OBGYN, she had witnessed more than a few unfortunate circumstances. She comforted me with some personal stories and assured me that I'd see sunnier days again in the future. "That's what happens to good people – good things," she reassured me with a knowing nod as she put a hand on my shoulder. I breathed in deeply, trying to internalize her wisdom and kindness. I hoped to use strength like hers to supplement my own.

We were now three weeks into therapy and trying our best to live in this new state of normal. "Do you want to get breakfast at Uncle Mike's?" he asked me one Saturday morning, as I was busy writing in my journal. I looked up curiously.

"Sure, I'd like that," I responded. It sounded like a good opportunity for us to talk about how we were both feeling. As we got into the elevator to go to the car, I looked at him carefully while he stared down at his own feet with his hands shoved in his jacket pockets. Maybe, I thought, just maybe he was having a change of heart. We took Dylan's car to breakfast, an almost identical Honda Pilot to mine (his was tan-colored, and mine was dark green). Heading north on Halsted, Dylan decided to play some music by Death Cab for Cutie and quietly sang along. I relaxed my head into the headrest and closed my eyes, imagining for a moment that we were still a normal married couple. As we headed west down Grand Avenue, Dylan started talking.

"I was looking at apartments in this area," he said, still tapping his hand along to the music. "I was hoping to find a place with a park nearby, so I could take the baby there. A place like that," he said as he pointed to an apartment building to our right, just half a block from a park with a baseball field.

"Do you mean for yourself or for us?" I asked.

"For me."

"So, you've decided how this is going to turn out?"

"I'm just considering options," he said, visibly annoyed. I took a deep breath and exhaled slowly, trying to slow the pace of my heartbeat as I fought off the feelings of anger and hurt. I decided to suck it up and keep quiet.

We pulled up to our usual breakfast spot. It was one of my favorite places to eat, and they served delicious Filipino food. We placed our order quickly, two plates of *tocino* (cured pork shoulder) with eggs over easy and garlic fried rice. I remained quiet while we waited for our food, my mind spinning a million miles an hour. *Why was he so excited about the thought of his own apartment? Why doesn't he consider an option where we end up happy together?* I wondered to myself as my emotions continued to churn inside my body. When the food finally arrived a few minutes later, I was barely two bites in when tears started streaming out of my eyes. I couldn't hold it in.

"Why couldn't you possibly imagine living with our baby and me with all of this daydreaming you've been doing?"

He put his fork down, "I don't know!" he snapped at me.

"I'm so hurt by all of this. I don't know what to do but tell you. I don't know what to expect in return."

"Well, great, now you've just ruined my meal," he said, with a mouthful of food. As he finished chewing, he threw his napkin over the plate. He stood up. "I'll be in the car," he said as he turned his back to me and walked out.

I continued to eat, my face hot with disappointment. *Why couldn't I just keep my cool and keep my mouth shut?* After a few more bites, I wiped the tears off my cheeks and asked the waiter for the check. I walked out of the diner, half expecting that he'd be gone. Our car was in the same spot, with Dylan sitting in the driver's seat, looking straight ahead with an angry grimace on his face. I climbed into the passenger seat and didn't say a word. Once we got home, I drove back to my parents' house to stay for the remainder of the weekend.

At work, I tried to resume a sense of normalcy. It was the one area of my life where I was excelling, and I didn't want to slip up. Somehow, I was able to dig deep and continue to contribute quality work for my client and even worked some late nights with my teammates Nilesh and Jerry, who were my main partners on the account. They were in my inner circle and knew exactly what was going on with my personal life but were kind enough to help keep my mind off of things and keep focused on our tasks. We had regular calls with our client, and, based on the feedback; we were meeting their every expectation. They were ready to move onto another phase of consultancy with us. Every day working with my team was another miracle to me.

Meanwhile, though, my heart stung like a rubber band snapped into it every time someone outside my tight circle at work would ask me the simplest questions: "Do you know if it's a boy or girl?" or "Do you have a name picked out?" or "You and your husband must be thrilled! When's the baby due?" I tried to hide the emotion on my face at these times, and I probably failed. The shame reached its peak one day when a potential customer came onsite for a full-day meeting. We were trying to close a large pharmaceutical client based out of Chicago, and they wanted to walk through a detailed roadmap of what to expect with a new PIM implementation using our services. Knowing this had become my forte, I walked into the meeting, ready to lead the client through the value proposition of what we do and what we had planned for them. *This will be a slam dunk*, I thought to myself. A middle-aged gentleman named Matt from the client-side, couldn't help but comment multiple times on my belly. "Wow, you look like you'll pop any minute!" he said, winking at me. I was sure he had good intentions, but anytime I would direct the conversation to our services, he'd insert another comment. "Do you tell your husband to get you what you're craving when you're hungry at night? I bet you're keeping him on his toes!" he said jovially. My face burned a bright red, and I almost lost it. *Fucking asshole! I don't actually have a husband – at least not one who gives a shit!* I wanted to say. I took a deep breath.

"Yes, definitely keeping him on his toes." I barely got the sentence out of my mouth. It was enough to make me want to crawl into a hole and die. Nilesh and I made eye contact, and he knew that Matt had pushed me too far. "Guys, I'm going to get us back on topic here," he said, turning the attention away from me. "I have a few points I'll walk you through that our team has outlined on our services value proposition …" He gave me a knowing look. He was going to cover for me. Grateful, I stood up. "If you'll excuse me," I whispered to no one in particular as I left the room, my hands on my stomach. "I need a break." I made a beeline towards the bathroom, where I stood sobbing for a good twenty minutes before I could recompose myself.

Marriage counseling with Meg continued. I'd bought Dylan a journal from the bookstore near work, leaving him a post-it note on the inside cover where I had written "To my best friend of the last decade…. Hope this journal leads you back to you. I can only hope it leads you back to us. No matter where it brings you, I wish you love." As the weeks passed, it felt like little to no progress was being made. We confirmed and re-confirmed over the next three sessions that Dylan was not sure how he was feeling, why he was feeling this way, and that he wanted more space.

After three weeks, my father-in-law Dan called me while I was at my parents' house. "Hi Vanessa!" he said in a cheerful tone. "Karol and I have been thinking about you and the baby. How are you feeling?" As he talked, I walked upstairs toward my bedroom and shut the door.

"Hey, Dad, thanks for calling," I said as I sat down on the bed. "We're doing okay, no more nausea, thank goodness!" It was so nice to hear his voice. Dan reminded me of Clark Kent's father from Superman, an all-around good guy whose moral compass was unshakable.

"Glad to hear it. Is now a good time to talk?"

"Yes, absolutely. Are you and mom okay?"

"Oh yeah, Karol's been traveling and didn't get a chance to call you sooner, so I thought I would. I've been busy with work as usual. And, well… I've been talking to Dylan every few days. I have to tell you I'm pretty frustrated with his answers. I can't understand what the problem is."

"I'm frustrated too. I don't know what else to do or say to help change things." It was nice to hear that Dylan's own father was in my corner on this.

"Have you looked around the condo to see what he's up to? Do you ever check his phone or look through his things? I mean, you deserve some answers, and you're not getting them." I was surprised by his suggestion.

"Well, no, I don't snoop around his things, not really. I've never checked his phone. There was one time I just checked his jacket pocket, and all I came up with was one of his classmate's business cards and some pink rock candy."

"Pink rock candy? That's interesting. Well, keep me posted if you find anything else. How has it been at therapy? Does your therapist have any insight on where you stand or where you should be now that you've been doing this for three weeks?"

"It's been slow going at therapy," I admitted. "Our therapist is really great, though. She's been pushing him to write in a journal, but I don't know how much effort he's really put into it. I guess I was hoping to see more progress by now. But, no, Meg hasn't given us any insight like that."

"Why don't you ask her next time you see her. Maybe she can suggest some milestones you should achieve in X number of weeks. I just want to know that you're heading in the right direction. I want him to love you, Vanessa. I'm having a hard time believing he doesn't."

Meg had been keeping me sane between marriage counseling sessions by starting to see me individually as well. She would meet me at lunchtime near work, or in the evenings over the phone while I was staying at my parents' house. When I approached Meg about my conversation with my father-in-law over lunch at Café Bacci, she paused for a minute before responding. "There's no defined timeline for something like this. I'm sorry I can't give you the answer you want. I know it's frustrating for you, and I feel the same." For the first time, I saw a hint of real emotion on her face. She wasn't kidding; she *was* frustrated, and the redness in her freckled cheeks confirmed it. I realized she was as human as I was. "What we are not getting are real answers. Dylan is just not giving them to you, me, or even himself. He's walking around lying to everyone, throwing away good things, and not owning up to his responsibility. That is my take on this. What I see in you, Vanessa, is that you are driven. You are a doer. You have a vision for what you want, and you take proactive steps to make them happen. I don't see him doing the same in his life. Somehow, in the midst of all of this madness, you were able to find me, and you were able to coerce Dylan to see me as well. It says a lot about your character. But you can't be responsible for all of this, especially for the things he is, or is not, doing. I want you to think about a word we've never talked about before. It's called co-dependency. Do you know what it means?"

"Not really," I admitted. I thought I was doing the right thing by fighting to keep my family together, especially with a baby on the way. "What does it mean?"

"Co-dependency happens when you put a relationship ahead of everything, ahead of your own needs and your health. Even the smartest people in the world can fall into co-dependent patterns. I just want to remind you that this relationship is not number one. Right now, you have to put yourself first. You have to be number one." The truth hit me like a slap in the face. I'd never thought of it in that way.

"Does this mean I should be filing for divorce?" Up until this point, I'd never said the word out loud to her, and it sliced through the air like a razor blade, ripping open a new possibility of giving up on my marriage.

"I can't tell you what decision to make, Vanessa. That's not how therapy works. I'm here to help you see the facts, help you come to your own conclusions, and hopefully help you find peace with whatever you decide." Even after all that she'd said to me today, I couldn't cope with the idea of giving up. I just wasn't ready.

Meg could see how much this new information was churning in me. Giving up on the relationship challenged some of my fundamental beliefs. Divorce was something foreign to my family, a major no-no in the Catholic Church. I didn't know how to reconcile it. *If I divorced, would God still love me? Would my parents think I was a failure?* I made a mental note to reach out to my pastor at St. Martha's to talk about it.

Meanwhile, Meg gave me a great suggestion of making a gratitude journal, which I latched onto. "Think of three things every morning that you're grateful for and write them down," she suggested. "This will rewire your brain to see the good in things instead of getting stuck on the negatives. And if your mind starts down a bad path, you can flip through it and remember the good things." Before we parted, she reminded me that I was a caring and deserving woman and asked me to honor myself throughout this process.

I applied what I learned from that conversation immediately. I started looking in the mirror every morning and saying to myself, "You are beautiful, and you've got this." Looking at myself in the eye and repeating this phrase felt awkward at first, but after a few days, I started to believe it. I looked for things to be grateful for and jotted them down in my journal whenever I felt inspired, which was surprisingly often. I was determined not to fall into a depression, and now that I had the tools to cope, I was going to make myself a better person than I was before.

One night at the condo, while Dylan was out with his friends, I was home alone with Rolo watching TV. I landed on ESPN, and it was in the middle of a special, introducing a popular new athlete to the basketball scene. He was a young man named Jeremy Lin. He had become an overnight sensation as a guard for the New York Knicks, yet he was an underdog. He was a Harvard graduate who was cut multiple times from the basketball team and seemed very unlikely to succeed at the level he had. Yet here he was, completely on fire, capturing the hearts of thousands, this Asian-American star. They coined it "Linsanity" which put a smile on my face. The story struck a chord in my heart. I talked to the baby growing in my womb, explaining the story to my belly. "We are the ultimate underdogs, Zach." One thing that Dylan and I had agreed right away on was the name of our son, Zachary Michael. "One day, my sweet, you'll be just like Jeremy Lin. We'll show the world just what we're made of, and you'll be a star." With all my heart, I imagined my son growing up to be someone so remarkable that he too, would make such an impression on the world. "Just like Jeremy Lin, baby boy," I whispered to him fondly, patting my belly. I went to sleep that night with a real smile on my face for the first time in a long time, dreaming about the wonderful person my son would become.

It was 6 pm on a Thursday, and Meg was about to arrive for our couple's counseling. This week we were focusing on understanding why Dylan felt the need to have more time for himself. "I decided that I need more time for myself to figure things out. I've been talking to one of my best friends, Josh, and he and I are planning a trip to Las Vegas. We're going in two weeks. It feels like the right thing to do, so I have my space," he proclaimed with authority, proud of himself for making such a decision.

"Our relationship is hanging by a tiny thread," I interjected, "we are weeks away from the baby's arrival and haven't sorted out what this will look like for him…and you think *now* is a good time to get away from it all? Do you even hear yourself? You sound so selfish!" This was the first time I'd found my voice in therapy.

"What the hell?" Dylan replied. "You think this is all about you?" He looked at me in disgust, his cheeks turning red.

"Now hang on…" Meg calmly asked him, "If Vanessa has moved out about half the week, and you're spending multiple nights each week hanging out with your friends, do you still not feel that you've had enough time for yourself?"

Dylan erupted in a way that I'd never seen before. "I need time away for *myself*– to think about *myself* for once! You two are just ganging up on me! You don't understand what I need here!" He threw his journal to the floor, near where Rolo was sitting, and the dog jumped up, startled.

"Dylan, no one is ganging up on you. *I'm* simply asking you how much more time you need for yourself, before addressing the issue of what is going on with your marriage and what your real feelings are. To be honest, from where I'm standing, it seems like you're running away from the problem instead of facing it. It's unfair to Vanessa, after all she has done to accommodate you. Have you ever considered that?"

To this, he stood up, red–faced, and screamed angrily at her, "You are *completely* on her side! This is *so unfair* of you!" He started sobbing, just like the night he told me he didn't love me. In between angry sobs, he continued, "This is such bullshit. If I say I need to get away, it's what I need for *me*! No one seems to care about what *I* need in this. Everyone just worries about *Vanessa*. Such *fucking bullshit*!" He slammed his fist into the top of the couch.

Meg stood up and looked at me. "Vanessa, do you have your stuff packed? I'd like you to leave with me tonight. I'll walk you to your car. It's not safe to leave you here with him. I'll wait while you collect your things. This session is over."

I was completely silent for a minute. *Was I really in danger with Dylan?* I'd never even considered that possibility. I'd known him to have a temper that would flare up on occasion, but this was really over the top. I finally responded. "Um, yes, I have my bag ready. I'm ready to go. I'm actually going to take the Halsted bus to Union Station. Are you taking the bus too?" I knew she lived north of us in the city. She nodded. I'd been doing so much living out of a duffle bag; I had a bag packed all the time. Hurriedly, I put on my coat. Meg and I closed the door and heard Dylan continue screaming and crying. I put my hand on the door, feeling his inner turmoil and wishing there was something I could do. But I felt helpless. *Am I a bad person for leaving him in this state?* I wondered to myself. She put her hand on my shoulder.

"It's okay to walk away. You are not responsible for this," she reminded me. The elevator doors opened, and as I stepped in, I felt like I was saying goodbye to the life I knew.

We stood on Halsted and 16th, waiting for the bus, and I looked up at our condo. Dylan was standing on the balcony, smoking and staring down at us. From a distance, it looked like he was amused. *How is he already calmly smoking a cigarette?* It was the first time I'd looked at him and felt afraid. Two minutes ago, he was screaming and sobbing at the door of our condo, and now he looked completely calm on the balcony. *Had he been acting in there, pretending to be upset?* I averted my eyes and looked down the street, waiting for the bus to approach. I felt bad for leaving Rolo at the condo and decided at that moment that I needed to move out permanently – and that I'd be taking Rolo with me. Part of me worried that Dylan might do something to hurt himself, so I sent a message to my father-in-law, asking him to check in with Dylan later that night.

Meg took a while to compose herself, telling me she needed a few minutes before she would be ready to talk. Her cheeks were bright red, and her body rose up and down as she took deep breaths. After a few moments of silence, I mentioned to her that I'd been praying the rosary every day, trying with everything in my heart to feel guidance from God. I'd spoken to my pastor, Fr. Dennis, a few times over the week, and he'd reassured me that I could go through a divorce and still be a devout member of the Catholic Church. He prayed with me and committed to help see me through this. He would even help me pursue an annulment should we proceed with a divorce. Just the other night, I'd looked at my rosary more closely, and miraculously, the links between the beads looked like they had turned from silver to gold. I took it as a sign that God was listening. I was keeping my heart completely open to receive guidance from Him.

Several days later, I was packing the last of my boxes. It was just a few days before my 33rd birthday, and Charmaine had met me at the condo to help me as the moving truck pulled in. "Did you take everything that's yours?" she asked me, scanning the living room full of boxes. She walked down the hallway and opened up the door to the guest bathroom and the second bedroom.

"For the most part, yes," I said. "I still have a few purses and bags in the bedroom closet. They were pretty high up, and I didn't feel comfortable climbing to get them."

"I'll grab them right now. Get a box ready." Within minutes, my collection of bags was neatly tucked into the final large box, and she taped it shut. Scribbling onto it with a sharpie marker, she said, "You ready to start your new life? This will be so much better for you, Ness." She tapped the box and lifted it up to stack it on top of the other boxes.

"Yes, I'm ready to be done with this place," I admitted. If I accidentally left anything behind, I knew I could come back while Dylan was in Las Vegas. He'd be gone soon.

As the movers finished taking all the boxes, the bed frame, and the office furniture, I took one final look at my beloved condo. So many of my hopes and dreams had been wrapped up in this place. I looked lovingly at my kitchen and thanked it for the many happy times it had held for me. I noticed I'd left all my magnets on the refrigerator and grabbed them, putting them into my purse. I left only one behind. It was a quote from Winston Churchill that said: "Never, Never, Never Give Up." Before I closed the door one final time, I tucked a photo of Dylan and me from a night out on the town with our friends under the magnet. I hoped that he'd return from Las Vegas, ready to fight to save our marriage, but I also knew there was nothing I could do about it if he didn't. Like Meg had coached me, it was not all my responsibility. I'd learn to find happiness no matter the outcome. Cradling my belly in my arms, I made Zach the same promise, "We'll be happy with our new life, no matter what. I promise."

Chapter 6: Starting Over

With my parents away on vacation to Europe for the next two weeks, I had the house to myself. After years of waking up to the sounds of the city, with the hustle and bustle of traffic just outside my bedroom window, it was a bit of an adjustment living in the quiet of the suburbs. I did, however, have my faithful companion, Rolo, with me, and he was truly enthralled with his new atmosphere. He would start early in the morning by running down the staircase and peering through the curtains in the living room. He'd barked incessantly at the squirrels in the backyard and pawed at the sliding glass door, begging to rush out. After a solid ten minutes of barking on the morning of my birthday, I yelled downstairs. "Okay, okay, Rolo, I'm *coming...*" I checked my phone. It was 4:50 AM.

"My new normal," I thought to myself, rubbing the sleep out of my eyes and looking up at the ceiling, noticing the gold-colored light fixture with four candle lightbulbs that had been there since I was a little girl. For a few seconds, a feeling of grief swept over me, and I closed my eyes. I was thirty-three, pregnant, husband-less, and living in my parents' house. *How had this become my reality?* Rolo's barking continued, and I was grateful to have no choice but to snap out of it. I took a deep breath and swung myself out of bed, caressing my belly as I got ready to face the day.

As I let him out into the backyard, still dark as the sun hadn't even risen yet, I made myself a cup of hot mango tea. The aroma of it woke my senses as I sat down at the kitchen table, staring at my hands wrapped around an "I Love You Grandpa" mug that my sister had made for my dad with photos of her kids on it. I sorely wished my parents were home. It was lonely in this large house without them. But they'd made their travel plans so far in advance; I wouldn't have wanted them to change their plans even if they'd asked me. I stood up and walked over to the refrigerator at the other end of the room and surveyed the food. I decided on some Hawaiian bread and cream cheese, and stood at the kitchen counter, peering out the window while I ate my breakfast. Seeing Rolo run fearlessly through the yard, I couldn't help but smile. After having been a city dog on a leash all these years, he'd finally found some freedom to move. *It must be so liberating*, I imagined. I wondered if I could find a way to feel the same, liberated from the confines of a relationship where I was not truly loved.

I thought back to three weeks ago, the first night I had decided to pack my bags and start staying at my parents' house part-time. On the way out, I'd grabbed Sonia Choquette's book "Your Hearts Desire: Instructions for Creating the Life you Really Want," which I had credited with helping me to manifest my current career path. I figured, at some point, these same instructions could help me to create the kind of relationship I truly desired. While my ego told me to fight for Dylan, something in me wondered if that was even possible anymore. I also grabbed an unread, newer book Sonia had written called "The Power of Your Spirit." The title in and of itself sounded like exactly what I needed. After tucking them safely into my backpack, I swung the straps around my shoulders and then attached Rolo's leash to his collar. "Come on, boy. We're going for a ride!" I told him cheerfully as he stood up and shook his head side-to-side, his ears flapping back and forth excitedly. I turned towards Dylan, who was standing at the end of the hallway, watching us get ready to leave. He hadn't looked at me in the eye for weeks, and it caught me off guard.

"We're ready to go," I said, surprised at the sound of my own voice. I actually *sounded* ready to leave him, though a slight twinge of sadness hung around the edges of my thoughts.

"Okay, I can help you to the car." He took the packed suitcase and also removed the backpack off my shoulders and slung it across one shoulder. "I got it," he told me.

"Thanks."

We went down the elevator together and through the front door, making our way across Halsted where my car was parked. Though it was chilly out, the air felt heavy. Without the normal windiness that I'd grown accustomed to in Chicago, we could hear the sound of our own feet clicking on the ground. Dylan opened the trunk of my car and put my belongings inside it, while I opened the door to the back seat, letting Rolo hop in. I turned to Dylan, and we stood facing each other on the sidewalk for a minute longer. Wearing his usual grey hoody and White Sox baseball cap, I admired him for what felt like the last time. He looked me in the eye again. I recognized a look of fondness intermixed with confusion and sadness. Neither of us knew the protocol for this moment. Instinctively, I reached out and hugged him, and for the first time since our lives had imploded, I felt him hug me back.

"I love you," I said with a tear falling down my cheek.

"Love you too."

"Goodbye."

Now, I heard a pawing at the door and dropped my Hawaiian bread on the plate in front of me, snapping out of my daydream. Sadness had started sweeping its way through my body quickly. I had read an article somewhere that said the baby could feel what its mother feels, and I desperately wanted Zachary to be happy. "I'm so sorry, baby boy, you will have a happy life, I promise you," I whispered to him as I slid the door open. I had Rolo's bowls of food and water ready for him, and he eagerly gobbled it up once he got inside. I patted his head as he ate. I allowed myself to shed a few quiet tears as I sat on the kitchen floor with Rolo. After a minute of this, I shook my head and clapped my hands, using brute force to snap myself out of it. It was my birthday after all, and it was no time to sit around, feeling sorry for myself.

I grabbed my cell phone and googled, "Father Peter Mary Rookey" the full name of the man of miracles who had helped me back in college. *I could use a little more firepower with my prayers,* I thought to myself. Fr. Rookey had a website and a form you could fill out with prayer requests. Within minutes, I'd spilled my heart out on this electronic form and left my cell phone number, so he'd be able to call me back later. *Help is on the way*, I thought to myself, relieved. I also found an online video of his Miracle Prayer that was accompanied by beautiful soothing instrumental music and some background information on his work. *This is the kind of soundtrack I wouldn't mind burning into my psyche*, I thought to myself as I favorited the link so I could come back to it easily. I was not going to let this birthday get the best of me.

I went back upstairs to take a shower and start my workday from home, which already put my mind at ease. I'd decided that once I moved, I would be kinder to my body and spirit than I'd ever been before. I had set up my bathroom to be a small sanctuary, with all my toiletries, including various scented body washes, lotions, and face masks lining the shelves invitingly. If I was going to be going through the heartache of a breakup, I might as well feel like I'm at the spa, I figured.

In my makeshift office, most of my photography gear was still in boxes, shoved in the corner of the room, but the desk was set up perfectly and felt a lot more spacious than it had in my old condo. "This is a good improvement, "I told the baby with a smile. I'd spent all weekend unpacking and had decided to convert my sister's old bedroom into my new bedroom, my brother's old bedroom into the nursery for Zach, and my old bedroom into the office in which I now sat. Though I was still sleeping on my sister's old mattress, I'd decided I would treat myself to a brand new comfy one within a couple of weeks. There was still a lot to finish up, but it was a livable situation for now. A few days earlier, I'd hired movers to transport all the existing furniture from the three rooms into a storage unit nearby so there would be enough space for all the things I was moving in. Within just a few days, each room looked completely different, and I was proud of how quickly I could convert the space when I put my mind to it. It was encouraging.

My phone buzzed around 8 am. "Happy Birthday, Ness! I hope you're having a good morning. Can you come over later after work? I'm making dinner for us, and Valentina picked a cake for you!"

"Thanks, Char! I will be there as soon as I can – I will call you later."

After a meeting with my client and a few internal calls with my team, I rolled back in my chair, stretched my arms overhead, and carefully rested both hands atop my belly. I stared out the window at the front lawn and the driveway, thinking about the many times Dylan and I had pulled up to my parents' house together. I knew he wouldn't be making an appearance today or anytime soon. I wondered about divorce and how people did it. I opened up my browser and searched *Chicago Divorce Attorney*. It returned a list so large that I didn't know where to begin. I was overwhelmed. *There has to be an easier way,* I thought to myself. I could think of only one person in my immediate circle who'd been through a divorce — Jerry. He was one of my closest colleagues. Without hesitating, I gave him a call. After just one ring, I heard him pick up.

"Hey, Vanessa, what's up?" he chirped quickly.

"Hey Jerry, I am glad you answered. I wanted to ask you for some advice. Do you have a few minutes?"

"For you, I do."

"Great… well, this is kind of awkward and completely unrelated to work. I know you've been through a divorce, and you're the only person I know who has walked the walk. I'm completely out of my element here," I said to Jerry honestly. "I'm fairly certain this whole thing I've got going with Dylan is going to end in divorce. I just want to make sure I'm doing the right things. Do you have any advice for me?"

"Vanessa, first of all, you should know, you're going to get through this just fine. If I know anything about you, I know you have balls the size of a rhinoceros."

I laughed out loud. He always had a special way with words.

"I've seen you conquer things in business that I didn't think you'd be able to, honestly. It's impressive. I don't see any reason why it would be different for you with this. The thing about divorce is, it feels like a death. You have to give yourself the time and space to mourn. I split from my wife after twelve years. I spent most of my adult life with her, and one day she was done with me. I mourned it like I would have if someone had died. After about three months, things started to get better. My life started to feel normal again."

What an interesting view on it, and how true it felt. It was the death of the life I once knew. "Thanks for the perspective," I replied. "It really does help. I am trying to figure out the logistics of all this. I've moved out of my condo - which I'm still paying for by the way - but I think I need to start looking into getting a lawyer. How did you figure this part out?"

"I had a lot of attorney friends," he responded. "But I'm in New Jersey. I don't know offhand of who in Chicago would be good. You'll want to find a winner – because you'll want to win big on this, Vanessa. You have that baby to worry about, and it doesn't sound like he's going to man up. If the guy were in New Jersey, I'd tell you this much… He'd be getting a major beat down by a group of guys who would *handle* this for you. Anyway, I'll find out for you on the attorney – let me make a couple of calls."

Relieved to have some help in my attorney search, I took a break for lunch and drove out to a nearby Panera Bread for a salad and sandwich. I pulled my laptop out so I could continue responding to emails as I ate. I started to lose myself in work again, feeling good about being an expert in this arena. An hour later, a text came through from Jerry with two solid referrals on Chicago based attorneys. Within minutes, I had appointments scheduled with each of them. I called my sister to make sure she could come with me to the appointments.

"Hey, Char... listen, I made a couple of appointments with attorneys."

"Are you filing for divorce? Have you decided?" She asked softly.

"Nothing's decided yet, but I need to be ready either way."

"Okay, that's good. These seem to be the right steps, and I'm with you. I'll make sure my schedule is clear for what you set up. But enough talk about this lawyer stuff for today, let's celebrate your big day!"

"Sounds good! I'll just grab my things and be over soon." I was so relieved to have my sister. She made everything in my life so much better, especially now. I headed back to my parents' house to drop off my work bag and head to Glenview.

As I made my way up the stairs, my phone buzzed with another text message, this time from Dylan. "Happy Birthday. I bought you a DVD player. I left it in the condo for you." My heart sank. Maybe it would have been better if he didn't text me at all. I was finding it harder and harder to bring myself to communicate with him. *What kind of gift is a DVD player? Was it thoughtful or just insulting?* I honestly couldn't tell anymore.

"Thanks," I responded. I took my phone and threw it into my bed, annoyed that I'd texted him back at all.

Within 15 minutes, I was pulling up into the driveway of my sister's house. I knocked quietly on the door, and my bright-eyed adorable three-year-old niece, Valentina, opened it with the biggest smile on her face.

"Hi, Tita! Happy birthday!" and she threw her arms around my legs. *Tita* means *Aunt* in Tagalog. I kneeled down to get closer to her and hugged her back.

"Thank you so much, sweet girl!" Her jet-black hair was pulled into pigtails, making her impossibly perfect face even more adorable. "I hope my baby boy is as sweet as you when he's your age. Now let's see, what did you and your mama make for dinner tonight?"

"We made steak! I bought a cake!" She exclaimed proudly. She had me grinning from ear to ear. This was exactly the kind of evening I needed.

"Hey, Vaness!" I heard my sister's voice coming from the kitchen. "I'm just finishing up in here. Want to help me set the table?" I walked down the hallway leading to the kitchen and admired the newly hung family photos they had framed and mounted to the wall.

"For sure!" I responded, heading down the hallway to grab some plates and silverware from the kitchen. "Great pictures, Char. I love how you framed them."

"Yeah, and we are going to hang up more photos in the upstairs hallway. The photos you took last year."

"Awesome. Is Lance home yet?"

"Not yet, in about 20 minutes." Charmaine and Lance had been a couple since college, and I truly admired their partnership. Lance was doing well in his career as a director of a boutique consulting firm.

When I arrived in the kitchen, I found about a half dozen helium balloons bunched together, a pale purple color, and one metallic one that said, "Happy Birthday!" on it. My sister emerged from behind the balloons to give me a big hug.

"Happy Birthday, Vaness!" she exclaimed, beaming at me. "You're 33! Three has always been your lucky number. That means it's going to be a great year! Liam's still having a nap upstairs..." As she pulled away to look at me, I broke into tears.

"I'm so sorry, I wasn't expecting much, this is so sweet of you, thank you. I don't know why I'm crying. I'm sorry!"

"Ness, it's okay! I'm sorry I made you cry. What did I say?"

"Oh, no, it's nothing you said at all... I'm just sad, I guess; I didn't think I'd be going through a breakup at this point in my life. Today really hurt, I mean I'm talking about divorce now like it's a real thing. I wonder if mom and dad will think I'm a failure." The thought of failing my parents hung over me like a black cloud. It was one of my deepest fears. I should have been better for them. I wiped the tears from my eyes, hurriedly. "Let me go wash my face off, and I'll be right back."

In their guest bathroom, I splashed cold water on my face. I was irritated by how much mood swinging I was doing today. One minute I was happy, and the next I was in tears. As I got a glimpse of myself in the mirror, all that registered was sadness. I had to fight this feeling off quickly, as I didn't want to spoil the evening. I put my hands on either side of the sink bowl and forced a smile on my face, just to see how it looked on me. *Fake.* I tried again, still looking quite contrived, and maybe a little crazy. The insane look on my face actually made me laugh, and that's when I realized I was getting the hang of it. "One step at a time," I told myself. "Tonight, you'll celebrate and be happy, that is the only goal."

After dinner, as Valentina had promised, she had picked out a beautiful cake for me with light purple frosting and "Happy Birthday Vanessa!" written in a deep royal purple. With a slice of cake and a tiny pour of red wine, Charmaine and Lance toasted me on my birthday, and I felt extremely lucky to be surrounded by family.

At about 8:15 pm, my eyes were starting to feel heavy. I excused myself and headed home, took Rolo for a quick walk around the block, and got ready for bed. Before any feeling of loneliness could creep in, I invited him to jump up on the bed with me, my body so tired that I fell immediately into a deep sleep.

My dreams were vivid again that night. This time I was wandering around in an unfamiliar run-down apartment complex in Chicago. There appeared to be some kind of party going on in one of the units, full of people who seemed to be in their 20's dancing and drinking. I was nervous as I stuck out like a sore thumb in the middle of a party like this. I held my belly protectively, hoping the party wasn't disturbing my baby's sleep. The people at the party didn't seem to notice me at all. I then wandered to a room in the back of the apartment, where the door was already open. Inside the room, it was very dark with no lights overhead. A standing lamp that had been dimmed in one corner of the room was the only light source. There were three men, all kneeling around a circular a coffee table, focused on a glass sphere that was placed in the middle of the table. They were murmuring to one another softly, and I couldn't make out what they were saying. As I took a few steps towards them, I got a closer look. There was smoke inside the sphere, and in the middle of it was a pink rock. There was a tube attached to the sphere, and the men were taking turns inhaling the smoke.

Suddenly one of the men looked up at me. I gasped. It was Dylan. His eyes looked bloodshot, and when he locked eyes with me, a look of rage washed over his face. He started screaming at me to get out and asked, "What the *hell* are you doing here?"

I backed out of the room, shut the door behind me and started running. I was running as fast as I could, scared for my life, hearing Dylan shout from behind me. "You have no right to be here!" I looked ahead and saw door leading to the stairwell. I reached toward it urgently, and with Dylan right on my tail, slammed it shut and pushed hard against it so that he wouldn't be able to open it. I felt him kicking the door, ready to force his way in.

I woke up in a full sweat and shaking. The baby inside me was kicking, probably not liking the adrenaline rush that this dream had given him. Trying to calm him down, I breathed slowly for about ten minutes before I attempted to get out of bed for the day.

Chapter 7: Switching Tracks

I started taking comfort in the ritual of my half-hour Metra train commute into the city, of sitting or standing in silence while, for the first time, really observing people around me. I mused about the professionals in business casual clothes busily typing away into their computers or texting on their phones. I often wondered what everyone else had going on in their lives. Were they, for the most part, happily married and in relationships? Was anyone going through a divorce like I was? Were any of them as uncomfortable in their skin as I was? Surely, I could not be the only one.

Nonetheless, I liked the anonymity of being a train rider. No one made eye contact, and no one judged. We all seemed to be in our own little bubbles.

Since I was a little girl, the train had always intrigued me. When I was seven years old, and on a family trip to New York, I'd gotten lost on the subway when I fell asleep during a ride. Somewhere in Midtown Manhattan, my parents had decided to exit, and my dad, whom I was sitting next to, hadn't noticed I was half asleep. My eyes shot open when I felt something was wrong, and I saw my entire family walking off the train. I jumped out of my seat and ran towards them, but it was too late – the doors closed right as I tried to step through them. My father had noticed at the very last second. I saw a look of panic come over his face as he tried to pry the doors open with his bare hands, to no avail. We started moving again, my family looking at me desperately from the platform as the train pulled away.

I knew I should have been scared, but at that moment, a warm calm came over me, and I knew everything was going to be just fine. An older man, whom I later referred to as my guardian angel, had noticed my predicament and stood beside me with his hand on my shoulder. He told me with a wink, "We'll get off at the next stop. Your dad will come for you there." In my seven-year-old mind, it would have made more sense to stay on the train that I was on. *Dad knows which train I'm on and he'll find me on it.* But I trusted this elderly gentleman instinctively. It was one of my first tangible moments of absolute trust in the universe, knowing that something bigger out there was watching over me. As promised, we got off at the next stop together and sat on a bench waiting. Fifteen minutes later (the most terrifying fifteen minutes of my mother's life), I was reunited with my family. Throughout the rest of that trip to New York, I felt I was having real conversations with God. I'd ask for signs — a particular bird formation in the sky or two dogs on a leash and a woman in a fur coat — and within seconds, I would see exactly that. It was too eerie to be a coincidence. I was onto something.

Now, at 33 years old, alone, pregnant, and on the train to work, I wondered where my guardian angel was. I thought back to the time when I first found out I was pregnant. It was the wee hours of the morning, and I'd asked Dylan to buy a pregnancy test on the way home the night before. I was feeling queasy, and we'd been trying, and I had a feeling this was it. To say I was excited was an understatement. I tried to wake him up to let him know I was taking the test, but he was too exhausted to get up. After peeing on a stick and waiting 3 minutes, the sign was positive. I thought Dylan would be as elated as I was, and as I ran back into the bedroom, screaming about the good news, he was upset that I'd woken him up. "I can barely open my eyes," he growled at me, annoyed.

It didn't register for me at the time that he wasn't happy about the pregnancy. Dylan and I had always told people we were on the "five-year plan." We wanted to travel, to see the world, and get everything we wanted to experience out of life done before we had a baby. And that is exactly what we did. Or so I thought. We'd traveled all over the US on trips with friends, to Mexico on romantic getaways, and to Europe for two weeks the previous summer. I grimaced to myself, wondering what else he wanted out of life if it wasn't this baby and me. Truth be told, I was angry that Dylan could continue to do whatever he wanted to do, and that I was stuck here in this very pregnant body, having to slow down and take on the responsibility of being a mother, seemingly all on my own.

I fantasized about the life I would have had if I had not been pregnant. In one scenario, I'd move to another country, start a new life somewhere in Europe, like France or Germany. I'd convince my company to relocate me to one of our European offices. I wanted that kind of career. I loved traveling! I'd find a handsome European man, and we'd live happily ever after. In another fantasy, I'd be living in a cool new apartment in Old Town, another great neighborhood in Chicago, drinking away the sorrows of my divorce but looking fabulous and finding all sorts of new men to date. In this fantasy, I'd be able to numb the pain away with cocktails and dancing. But alas, I could not run away to Germany or France, or even to Old Town for that matter. I was having a baby in a few weeks, and I needed to get my act together. There was a tiny companion with me now at all times, counting on me to do the right thing for us. There was nowhere to run but inward. I had to resolve my heartbreak head-on, completely sober.

The train creaked and screeched as it made its final turn towards downtown Chicago. "Next stop…Union Station…"

That announcement was my gentle reminder to come back into my body and start thinking about work again. My client was just starting their PIM software implementation, and I had a team to lead on the vendor side for another few weeks, along with a transition to plan for while I was out on maternity leave. I got right to business once I got into the office, cranking out project plans and scheduling meetings for the next several hours.

At around noon, a reminder popped up on my screen "Massage: 12:20" It was the third Thursday of the month, and I had my appointment set up with Gianna, a massage therapist who came to our office regularly. Gianna had become a friend over the years, and she was up to speed on the latest on-goings in my life. She'd been through a traumatic divorce herself many years ago, and she could relate to so much of what I was feeling. It was such a relief to have a girlfriend who'd been there, done that.

"Hi, Gianna!" I said as I walked in, inhaling the lavender fragrance that she must have sprayed in the room. Gianna was a lovely lady in her forties with shoulder-length brown hair and a contagious smile. She had been doing bodywork for decades and was so in tune with mind-body-spirit connections, that our conversations always ended up on the topics of spiritual growth, healing, and self-reliance.

"Hello, my sweet!" she responded back with a sunny smile on her face as she gave me a big hug. "You look adorable! How is that baby doing?"

"The boy is alive and kicking!" I motioned to my baby, putting her hands on the left side of my belly so that she could feel his current movements.

"Wow, would you look at that!" she exclaimed.

She started to work on my feet and calves, which had needed the most attention lately. We avoided any work near my lower back so that we wouldn't cause any premature contractions.

"I was thinking…" she said carefully, "with everything you're going through and the amount of healing you want to accomplish before this baby is born… There's someone I want you to see. Her name is Donna, and she is a Reiki Master, and honestly, a great therapist. I think her healing modalities would blow you away. I've been seeing her for years, and she's amazing."

"If you think that highly of her, count me in." I would do anything to expedite this pain out of my heart. I jotted down Donna's information and left her a message later that day. Something inside me told me to be very excited about meeting with her. I prayed on it on the train ride home.

The next evening, Lance drove Charmaine and me back to Pilsen. I'd asked them to come to the condo with me while Dylan was out of town to grab a few last items. Walking into my condo again with a fresh set of eyes, I felt a nervousness coming over me. The magnet and photo I'd left on the refrigerator were still there, and my flamenco paintings were still hung on the wall of the living room. But the energy here no longer belonged to me. I was an outsider. I couldn't shake the nervous energy, nor could I explain why my heart was beating so fast. An irrational fear came over me that Dylan was going to show up any second, though I knew he was still in Las Vegas.

"Let's make this quick, I don't like the feel of this place anymore," I told them.

Lance pulled my paintings off the wall while Charmaine and I headed into the master bedroom. I headed straight into the bathroom and started going through the cabinets. I was missing my favorite Smashbox eye shadow and knew it had to be here somewhere. I sat down on the floor to have a better look, and in one of the drawers, there it was. Relieved, I put it into my purse and started to get up to join Charmaine back in the bedroom when a strange scent entered my awareness. "Char, can you come in here?"

"What's up?" she said, walking into the bathroom.

"I smell something, do you smell it? I think it smells like pot."

I reached over to Dylan's side of the sink, and within seconds, I was pulling out a large Ziploc, full of smaller Ziploc bags, each one packed with marijuana. I also found a small wooden box with a cigarette shaped contraption inserted into it. I knew it wasn't used for smoking nicotine. I was stunned.

"What the fuck?" I said out loud to myself. My whole body got hot, and I took a deep breath. I had no idea he smoked anything besides cigarettes. I thought back to a time where he'd taken a trip with his friends and had smoked weed, but he'd assured me it was a one-time thing that they tried for fun. I wondered what else he was doing that I wasn't aware of. Thoughts of the pink rock candy, and my dream came flooding back into my mind, and I realized that my subconscious was telling me more than I was willing to believe at the time. I put my hand over my belly protectively.

"Lance!" Charmaine yelled down the hallway. "Can you come here? Vanessa just found drugs."

Without pausing, I took each little baggie and dumped it into the toilet, while shaking my head. I felt a new sense of fear building for my unborn son. *Would he be safe with his father? How could I protect him from this?* There was so much I apparently did not know about Dylan. Anger was simmering in my body, and my hands were shaking.

"Wow, he is extremely disappointing. I had no idea he was into this…" I heard Lance say as I flushed the toilet. He and Charmaine continued to talk, and I walked back into the bedroom. There was so much turmoil churning in my body, I could barely comprehend their words anymore.

"Let's get out of here. I've seen enough," I said as I took the laptop by Dylan's bedside. It was technically my laptop that I'd bought for my photography business, and I was no longer feeling charitable. As we headed past the kitchen towards the front door, I pulled the magnet and photo off of the refrigerator, tore the photo into pieces, and threw them in the garbage. On the drive home, I flipped open the laptop and within minutes had found an alarming amount of pornography and gambling websites. I was sick to my stomach. *Damn.* I really didn't know him *at all*.

From that moment on, I switched tracks. Instead of fighting like hell to save my marriage, I decided I would fight like hell to secure my son's safety and establish my own independent identity. Later that evening, I wrote Dylan an email, one that I'd decided would be my final communication for as long as humanly possible.

Dylan,

I have decided to file for divorce. You will be hearing from my attorney, Helen Sawyer, in the next few days. I have found her to be fair and reasonable and trust that she can get us through this divorce amicably.

Meanwhile, I am no longer paying for your cell phone bill. I've called AT&T to cancel your number from my plan. You have 48 hours to contact them to claim the number and set up your own plan.

Please do not contact me directly going forward. Any and all conversations can be managed through Helen, whom you will have contact information from very soon.

Regards,

Vanessa

The finality of it made me feel like I'd just dived into the middle of the ocean without knowing if I could swim. As terrified as I was, I found anger to be an unexpected friend. I embraced it. It gave me enough strength to handle the transaction with my new attorney, and enough bravado to put on a courageous face in front of my family and friends. *I'm totally fine! I'm a strong, beautiful woman who deserves better! I'm lucky to be losing that loser!* The anger also gave me the gusto to call an old friend, Seth, who was a private investigator in Las Vegas, to see if he could help me get some answers about my soon-to-be ex-husband, along with any tangible evidence about that would help me to protect my son if I needed to.

"Seth, I can't believe I'm asking you to do this. Dylan just so happens to be in your hometown the next few days with one of his buddies, Josh. He's been hiding so much from me I just want to understand how far this rabbit hole goes and if my son is going to be in danger being with his father when he's born," I explained. "I found a bunch of weed at my house, and while I know that it's only weed… I have a strong feeling that he's doing harder drugs than that. I'm scared for my son."

"Okay, Vanessa, don't worry. I'll gather as much intel as I can. Give me all the details you know about this trip, a few recent photos of him and his friend, and I'll get back to you in a couple of days."

"Thanks, Seth. Can you do me a favor? Give everything you find to Charmaine so she can filter it down to what I need to know. I'm at an emotional exhaustion threshold, and I need to protect the baby."

"You got it, Vanessa. Take care of yourself and that baby. Let me know if you think of anything else that I can do to help you."

I prayed another rosary, with a special intention of protecting Zach with everything in my power. *Please, God, please help me to be enough for him. Help me to be strong enough to be everything he needs.*

At work on Monday morning, my phone rang as I was walking towards the office.

"Hi, is this Vanessa?" a woman's calm voice asked.

"Yes, it sure is. Is this Donna?"

"Yes, I'm so glad I caught you. I've been hearing your name as I was praying this weekend, and I wanted to call you sooner. Sorry, I was away for the weekend with my kid visiting a college..."

"No worries. Did you say you *heard* my name?"

"Yes, sometimes that happens when someone really needs my help. My angels will give me a little nudge to let me know about it. I get a lot of requests for appointments, and I can't actually fit everyone into my schedule. But I knew I needed to meet with you specifically."

I was intrigued. "Well, I could certainly use some prayers and some guidance. Gianna told me all about you, and I wanted to get together with you as soon as possible. I can take a day off work on Friday if that works for you?"

"That seems like divine timing. I have an opening on Friday at 11:30." She gave me her address, and we were set.

Every day after work that week, I focused on getting the house settled for Zachary and me. I decided to use my creativity to help me heal, creating the most beautiful environment I could for myself and my baby. Enlisting my sister's help, I made multiple stops to the local Home Depot, Bed Bath and Beyond, and Home Goods. I picked out a rich purple paint for my bedroom walls. I also bought a new mattress, complete with remote control and mechanism that could elevate the head of the mattress as high as I wanted. I treated myself to new lavender-colored sheets and a duvet with a lilac and white floral design. Then I focused on creating a gorgeous nursery for my son. I bought custom wall stickers for the nursery that spelled out "Zachary" in flowing cursive just above the crib, along with a beautiful tree design that took up most of the wall. I picked out new window dressings, light fixtures, and paint colors for my son's room. I talked to a family friend to help us redesign the closets in all three of the rooms to make them more functional. I was so grateful for the productive distraction – it indeed kept my heart from aching.

As we were hauling in the last of the bags from Home Depot in on Thursday night, Charmaine started talking about the private investigator's results. "Vaness, I got the report back from Seth. Let's talk about what he found."

"Okay," I said and let out a big sigh. I didn't want my mood to deflate but knew I had to face facts at some point. "Anything useful in there that I need to know about?"

"Well, all he witnessed for certain is that Dylan was gambling a *lot* with Josh, they'd go back to the bedroom frequently, and Dylan was not wearing his wedding band at any point."

I sat in silence for a minute, wondering if I should be upset. "Okay, it doesn't sound like much, but maybe it's enough just to have the peace of mind that I tried my best to get as much information as I could."

"There is something else Seth mentioned. He said he had a really hard time recognizing Josh from the pictures you sent. He had to get in really close to confirm that it was him; he looks so much thinner and doesn't look well. Seth said if he had to guess, Josh is a drug addict. He thinks they are both doing some serious drugs and that that's why they kept going back to the room. He studies people for a living, and this is his professional opinion. He just doesn't have any concrete evidence. Let me just see what else he wrote up…" She scrolled through some emails on her phone.

My blood was getting hot with frustration. "Well, this officially sucks...But there's nothing I can do about it without any evidence. I'll talk to my attorney to get some advice." I responded.

"Sounds like a good idea," she said, still looking intently at her phone with her eyebrows furrowed. "Hmmm..."

"What are you looking at?"

"It's strange... I just got this weird email on your photography page on Facebook." When I was more actively doing photoshoots, my sister helped me start a Facebook fan page, and I'd been fielding new requests from there. Since I was so busy at my day job, Charmaine had offered to be the moderator for the page and answer any messages that came in.

"What is it about?"

"He says his name is Dean and that he needs to speak with you about your husband. He left his phone number. Let me forward this to you."

I decided not to call back that night and let myself sleep on it. I wasn't sure I wanted to talk to anyone else about Dylan.

The next morning, I took the day off work and headed to Frankfort, a south suburb of Chicago, to meet with Donna. Pulling into her driveway, I noticed she had an angel statue near her front entrance. As I walked up the path towards her front door, she opened it and stood in the doorway. Her hair was a strawberry blonde with a pixie cut, and she had hazel eyes and a bright smile.

"Hi, Vanessa! Welcome, welcome! You've had a long drive to get here, please come in!" she said cheerfully as she motioned me inside.

"Hi, Donna! It's so nice to meet you finally."

She walked me into her house and invited me to pass through the French doors that lead to her workspace. In the middle of the room was a massage table with a pillow and a folded blanket on it. To the right of it against the wall was a bookcase full of various items, including oils, fragrances, chimes, bowls, and a small speaker that was currently playing some soft angelic-like tones. On the other side of the room was a large window with partway open blinds, letting daylight stream into the office. Donna invited me to have a seat in one of the two chairs facing each other next to the window.

"It's so peaceful in here," I noted. There was something about the vibe in here that made my soul feel invited and safe.

Donna smiled at me. "I cleared the energy in here before you arrived so you could feel safe and loved. There are angels all around you, and I can see the energy of your baby! He is so happy you are his mother!"

I looked up, quizzically. "How can you tell?"

"I can see your energy field, or as I like to call it, a bubble. You've got a very big one around you, and I can see your baby's bubble too. You've got a double-bubble," she said with a chuckle. "It's adorable, and your son can't wait to be out here in this world with you! He chose you; you know."

"Wow, that's incredible!" I said, truly interested in what she was seeing and how she was seeing it. "Well, listen, I'm not certain how all of this works. I am very open-minded and going through the hardest time of my life, as you know. I'm here because it feels right to be here, I'm hurting more than I ever have before, and I know I need to dig really deep to get through this. I was born and raised Catholic…my sister told me this might be against our religion… to be honest, I'm not sure I care about that right now. But I just wanted some perspective on that. I'm sorry in advance, but I'll probably be asking a lot of questions as we go through this."

"Oh, no worries at all. I understand. I am Catholic, too, and have done work with nuns at Catholic Churches. I've done work with other religious groups as well. I see this work as something that can help anyone regardless of religious affiliation. I can see energy and help you get back into balance, which is something you really need right now. Just relax, and we will get started. Let's take a few breaths together. You can close your eyes or leave them open, whatever makes you feel comfortable. I can see the sadness in your heart. I have some tissues here for you in case you need to cry. You don't have to hold back."

I closed my eyes and inhaled deeply. We started talking, just like it was any other therapy session. I gave her background on who I was, what my story was today, and I would hear her pausing to breathe. When I peeked my eyes open, I'd see her gazing over my right shoulder, nodding, and seeming to motion with one of her hands while exhaling, like she was energetically moving things around for me. I could feel a light airiness in my body the longer this went on. Eventually, she walked me over to the massage table and helped me up. As I laid down and closed my eyes, she hovered her hands over my heart.

As she continued to breathe deeply, she interjected softly. "I want you to know something. You do not need to feel ashamed. Why is there so much shame here?"

My heart started beating faster. "Because... I was supposed to know better. I am smarter than this. I'm ashamed... that I had no idea... my husband didn't love me." I was choking on my words. Tears flooded my eyes, and as I closed them, they streamed down the sides of my face. I let them flow, and they kept on coming. My body was trembling.

"Just breathe and relax...let go of the shame. It's not yours to carry." I laid in silence, letting the shame work through my entire body. I could literally feel it releasing from my heart center. After a few minutes, my body settled down, and my breathing steadied. I heard some beautiful chimes sounding over me, and I could smell a light citrus fragrance in the air. I felt wonderful.

"Okay, my dear, your energy is balanced. When you're ready, open your eyes. Take your time." I laid there for another few minutes, and when I was done, I opened my eyes and saw her smiling above me. "There you are... You are ready and strong. You can *do* this." It was an incredible feeling.

I was buzzing on the way home. I could not believe how helpful Donna was in the short time she'd worked with me. We had talked about the message that Dean left for me during our session. She said it would be eye-opening to hear from him but that I shouldn't pressure myself to do it if I didn't want to. Mulling it over, I decided to try calling Dean's phone number on the long drive. After a few rings, it went to voicemail. I felt slightly relieved. *Guess it wasn't meant to happen now.*

I was all smiles by the time I arrived at Charmaine's house later that afternoon. I practically skipped through the front door, beaming.

"I'm so glad you did it, Vaness," she said, giving me a big hug.

I smiled back, "Yeah. I have a long way to go, but I know I can do it." We sat on the couch in her living room while the kids watched one of their favorite shows, the Fresh Beat Band. I tapped my foot to the theme song, finally feeling like I could enjoy music again. Leaning my head back into the couch, I cradled my belly, explaining my "double-bubble" to my sister and feeling amazing. The universe always took care of me. I was sure of it.

That evening, vivid dreams flooded my sleep. I was a mom to a sweet, baby boy. I held him in my arms as we walked through a crowd of people at a carnival. Once we got past them, we made our way into an open field, and I laid down a blanket on an empty patch of grass. I carefully put my baby down to sit on it. He was old enough to hold himself up while sitting, his chubby hands grabbing pieces of the grass as he drooled. I put a bib around his neck and kissed his cheeks. The sun was setting, and we were getting ready to watch the fireworks on the 4th of July. I became aware that someone was sitting with us on the blanket, someone I cared for deeply. I handed him the baby. I couldn't quite make his features out, but he held the baby in his arms as he laid on the blanket, and Zachary was climbing up to rest his head on his chest. I laid next to this man, watching the sky light up into a bright combination of reds, purples, and blues, losing myself in the magic of the evening. I was happier than I had ever been.

Happy tears filled the corners of my eyes as I woke up the next morning. It felt good to be loved, if only in a dream. I spent the morning daydreaming about it while I started making a dent in the pile of books that had arrived earlier in the week.

In the middle of the afternoon, my phone rang. It was the number I had tried to call yesterday. *Dean.* I froze for a second. *Did I really need to talk to him?*

"Hello?"

"Hi. My name is Dean. I think you tried to call me yesterday." He sounded young, and I could hear a hint of desperation in his voice.

"Yes, I did. I think you sent me a message on my Facebook page… My name is Vanessa. Did you need to tell me something?" My heart was racing. I wasn't sure I wanted to know what he had to say, but I'd come too far.

I heard him sigh on the other end. "I… wanted to ask you about Dylan."

I cut him off. "I don't know much about him, actually. I haven't spoken to him in weeks."

"Okay, well, I think maybe you should know about your husband. He's been sleeping with my wife, Jessica."

I remained silent. My stomach was swirling, and I started taking deep breaths quietly. My cheeks were hot. Tears started welling up in my eyes again; only this time, they were tears of anger.

"They were in acting class together a few months ago. They started hanging out. And about a month ago, my wife came clean to me." His voice was shaky.

"Are you okay?" I asked quietly. After all the zen I'd created in my life up until this point, I felt like it was all crumbling around me yet again.

"I am having the worst time of my life. Did you have any idea this was going on?"

"No, I had no idea whatsoever. Thank you for shedding some light on where I had no information before. Dylan broke up with me out of nowhere a couple of months ago but never told me the truth of what he was really doing. I guess I know now." I paused to think for a minute. "Did your wife move out? Maybe she's been staying at my condo with him, in Pilsen. I packed up and left a few weeks ago."

"Yeah she was gone a few nights. I'm betting that was where she was." My blood was boiling. With my photo on the fridge, she had the audacity to stay in the home I was paying for and sleeping in the bed that I bought.

"What are you going to do? I filed for divorce. There was no marriage to save, and I need to move on."

He sighed. "Jessica is begging for me to stay with her. I guess she changed her mind about Dylan. She threatened to kill herself if I left her. To be honest, I'm pretty pissed off; she didn't even give me a chance to be mad at her. She held a knife to her wrist while she was telling me about the affair and was sobbing on the floor. I don't know what I'm supposed to do, but I don't want her to kill herself."

"Wow, Dylan was pretty dramatic too, sobbing on the floor when he told me he didn't love me. I wonder if they practiced that in an acting class," I said smugly. "At least she had the decency to tell you the truth. Dylan never has and probably will never tell me what was really going on. And all that while I'm pregnant with our first baby."

"Wow. I didn't know. I'm sorry this happened to you," he said. "You seem like a decent person."

"Thank you, and I'm sorry this happened to you, too."

Once again, anger was bubbling up inside me, along with a massive irritation that I'd ever even tried to work things out with him in the first place. He was playing me from the start.

Beyond a shadow of a doubt, the divorce was now the only path that made sense for me.

Over the next weeks, I let my home in Pilsen go into a short sale, my previously squeaky-clean financial status crumbling around me. So much of my identity had been tied to being perfect: having a perfect financial record, a perfect marriage, a perfect body, and a life that looked good on paper. I was learning to surrender to the truth that none of those things were actually me. They were temporary; none of them defined who I really was in my core. My worth was not tied to my marriage, my credit score, my physique, or other people's opinions of me.

The last few days of my pregnancy I held onto a quote from Sonia Choquette's book *The Answer is Simple*: "Even during the darkest night of the soul, the most self-loving and self-healing choice you can make is to keep your heart open and expect something good to come from your difficulties."

Chapter 8: The Arrival

On a hot summer evening, the day before my due date, I drove to the Glen, a popular area in Glenview that had small shops and a movie theater. Just east of the development was a park with a walking trail and a small man-made lake. I'd probably seen a half dozen movies at the Glen in the last two weeks, seeking both a mental escape and air-conditioning. My home was as prepared as it was going to be for the baby, I'd read myself into oblivion, and I was at the point where my belly was so huge, I was desperate to get labor moving along.

With the sun just starting to set, it had cooled down just enough for me to walk past the shops and toward the nature walk area. I saw two little children playing with their shoes off, splashing in a fountain at the Gallery Park, an open area just at the edge of the lake, where the walking trail began. The children's parents were sitting on a nearby bench, smiling at them and taking pictures. Their little squeals as the water splashed around them put a smile on my face, reminding me that one day my son would be doing the same. I started walking down the path, leaving the background noise behind me. Soon, I began to pick up the sounds of crickets and the smell of the grass in the air. It was peaceful. Wearing the most comfortable sneakers I owned, I plodded forward with swollen ankles, holding my belly up with my hands as I attempted to move quickly enough elevate my heart rate. My back ached slightly, but I was enjoying the movement, hopeful that it would woo my baby into labor. I rounded a part of the trail that had an opening very close to the water's edge. I decided to kick off my shoes and sit for a while, gingerly setting my heavy frame onto the side of a large rock.

I'd taken a magnifying glass to my soul over the past weeks, examining all the relationships I'd had over the years. I realized this was not the first time I'd been betrayed by a boyfriend; in fact, I'd had a habit of being with men who were ultimately unfaithful. My first serious boyfriend in high school had cheated on me just before senior prom, and I'd played the role of the victim back then. Another boyfriend I'd had as I started college had been into drugs. He blew me off steadily, and I'd turned a blind eye to it until I couldn't anymore. Why had I accepted that treatment? Why hadn't I had higher standards for myself during my adolescence? What it boiled down to was that I never truly believed that I was good enough. It took me all these years to realize this about myself, and it set off another wave of self-shaming.

I'd received multiple emails from Dylan's new attorney in the past weeks, calling me "manipulative and damaging" due to the fact that I'd taken Dylan's laptop, demanding that I buy him a new one. He was also threatening to come after me for alimony and claiming that I did not need child support, citing ways in which I had prevented Dylan from making a larger income during the time we were together. It was beyond insulting and incensed me to the core. His words were like little darts shooting at my heart, chipping away at any sense of pride that remained as I tried to hold my composure in my final weeks of pregnancy. *Doesn't this attorney have a heart at all? Doesn't he care how upset he's making the baby and me?*

I'd seen Donna multiple times by now, frequently feeling like I was hanging by a thread.

"Think of it as his attorney just checking the boxes on his to-do list," she advised. "This is what he does for a living. He does this *all the time* with all his clients, without any emotion. Don't invest any emotion back into it. Your angels want you to know that you haven't done anything wrong. While the words are hurtful, they are also untrue. You are safe..."

At Donna's suggestion, I spewed my anger onto the pages of my journal. I would then promptly rip out and burn the pages. I had done this ritual almost every night since she told me about it. I found the process to be intensely cathartic.

Dylan and his attorney had agreed to drug testing after stalling for several weeks, complaining about how ridiculous I was for asking for it in the first place. I'd offered to pay for all the testing, and for it to be done twice. I assumed Dylan was going on an intense detox, and though at times the revenge in me wanted to find him completely guilty and have the results come out positive, I also hoped he was cleaning up his act, and getting ready to be a father. There was a part of him I used to love, and though I would never want to be with him again, I wanted him to be the best person he could be, for the sake of our son. When the tests came back negative for drugs, I was reminded of what I'd read in *A Course in Miracles:* "Every decision I make is a choice between a grievance and a miracle." I chose the miracle.

Now, I ran my hand along the edge of the rock I was sitting on and felt a few pebbles. I picked two of them up and held them in my hand. The edges were jagged, imperfect. *Exactly as intended,* I thought to myself. I closed my eyes, sending a prayer out to the universe to help me to be 100% ready for motherhood, to be the best person I could be as I ushered this little life into the world, and to not ever to be defeated by anything that this divorce was imposing upon me. "The universe always has my back," I whispered to myself. I threw the pebbles as far as I could into the lake, feeling as giddy as a child throwing a coin into a fountain while making a wish. I heard them splash into the water, though I could barely see where they landed in the near dark. I patted my belly. "I'm ready when you are, baby." I stood up and made my way back to the car.

At 4 am the next morning, exactly on my due date, I awoke in my bed at my parent's house, to a wincing pain in my abdomen. Clutching the side of the bed, I took some deep cleansing breaths as the contraction hardened and slowly released. I'd rehearsed this routine in my head many times, but nothing prepared me for this level of excruciating pain. My black Puma duffle bag was at the side of my bed, packed with the essentials: a few comfy outfits to last me 2-3 days, dry shampoo, my favorite toiletries, my journal, and a sweet-smelling aura soma scent that Donna had given me to keep me calm while in labor. Once I had the wherewithal to grab my phone, I dialed my sister's number.

"Hello?" she said in a groggy voice.

"Hi Char, it's me. It's time."

Suddenly wide awake, "It's time?" she said urgently. "Okay, okay, I'm coming, give me twenty minutes, I'll be right there." She hung up.

I suddenly realized I was starving. Knowing that the hospital would not let me eat anything once I was admitted, I walked down the stairs slowly, and the contractions started up again. "Oh, God, please give me the strength…" I said out loud. I couldn't believe the next contraction hurt even more than the first.

I hobbled to the kitchen and grabbed some crackers, cheese, and a Sprite. After a few bites and a sip of my drink, I realized I was in too much pain to keep eating. I forced down one last bite before I decided to wake my parents up.

"Mom? Dad? I'm having contractions. I'm having the baby today."

My mom's eyes opened wide. "Oh, my *God*, okay, anak. What time is it? Is Charmaine already on the way?" she asked as she pulled herself to a seated position on the bed.

"It's about 4:15, Mama. Yes, she's coming now. Can Dad bring my bags downstairs? This hurts really bad."

My dad got out of bed quickly and walked over to me, putting his arm around my waist. "Okay, baby, it's time. I will bring your things downstairs. Let me help you down there first." He walked with me, and I squeezed his hand as the next contraction began.

"Dad, this hurts!" I said with tears streaming down my face.

"I know, baby, you'll be okay." Somehow, the confident tone of his voice convinced me I would be.

My parents stood outside with me in the driveway until Charmaine pulled up in her SUV. They would meet us at the hospital later, as I'd likely be in labor for several hours and having Charmaine with me was all I needed for now. She rolled down the passenger side window to talk to us. "Hi Vaness, are you okay?"

"Not really," I winced. "We need to get to the hospital quick. I'm in a lot of pain."

My parents moved quickly, throwing my bags into the backseat while I climbed into the passenger side. Before she closed my door, my mother shoved a brand-new rosary in my hand. "God bless you, mahal!" I could hear her say as my sister drove off.

"Oh... my... God...." I wrapped my hand around the door handle and squeezed it with all my might.

"Just take deep breaths, Vaness... we will get there soon.... When do you think I should text Dylan?" Just two days ago, our attorneys had finally hammered out a mutually acceptable agreement detailing what was to happen the day I went into labor. As part of the agreement, I needed to tell him when I went into labor. I was in far too much pain to text him myself.

"Let's just tell him...once we get there," I responded faintly as I squeezed the door handle again. *God, please, I need more strength...*

We exited on Ohio Street, and Charmaine navigated the downtown streets swiftly.

"Hang on, be there in a second, okay?"

"Okay..." I closed my eyes for a few minutes, breathing as deeply as I could, and by the time I opened them again, we were pulling up to Prentice Women's Hospital just off of Superior Street.

"We're here. Let's do this," she said confidently, jumping out of the driver's seat and running around the car to open the door for me.

Charmaine helped me to a seat in the waiting room, putting my bags next to me, and checked me in with the receptionist. "We need to move this along, and she needs an epidural," she said urgently.

"Yes, ma'am, but we need to make sure we get the paperwork right."

I spoke up from my seat. "I have a court order. I need to make sure you abide by this, please." Hands shaking, I reached into my purse and found it neatly tucked into the back pocket. Charmaine came over and grabbed it.

"They can keep this copy," I reminded her. I'd made five copies of it just in case multiple people needed to see it. The court order made it clear that Dylan was not to enter the room while I was in labor. That was one sticking point I wouldn't waver on. I wanted to have the baby in peace. I didn't want more drama while I was trying to deliver my son. The court order also gave Dylan the right to visit the baby in a separate room as soon as reasonably possible under the supervision of one of the hospital workers.

When I got situated in a hospital room, I was informed there were six mothers ahead of me, also being confirmed and admitted. I nodded in understanding, while my sister asked if she could speak to the nurse outside. She was persistent as ever, trying to expedite me ahead of the line.

Charmaine walked back into my room. "Hey, they are going to see you really soon. I have to get my car into the parking lot. I'll be right back. She dug her hand into my purse and fished out my phone, putting it in my hand. I realized I was still holding the rosary too. "Call me if you need me. I will only be a few minutes, I promise. Deep breaths…" and she ran off.

A nurse came in to see me and asked me to change into a hospital gown and give her a urine sample. She gave me a hospital bag to put my clothes in. As I came in from the bathroom down the hallway, I set the bag aside next to the rest of my things on the floor.

"Perfect," she said, "Let's get you on this bed." She motioned me to use the stool next to the table to help me climb up. She had positioned the bed most of the way up like I was sitting in a recliner. Before I could get too comfy, she did a routine check for vitals, checking my blood pressure and temperature. She then strapped a wide belt across my stomach and back.

"This will help me measure your contractions, okay?"

"Sure. Another one is starting," I said, letting my breath out slowly and painfully. "They are getting really intense. How much longer before I can get an epidural?"

She offered me her hand. "It helps when you have a hand to squeeze during these," she said kindly. "We just need to confirm you're in labor officially. The doctor will be in shortly to do that, I'm just helping to get all your information ready for him, and once he confirms, we move you into L&D. From there, an anesthesiologist will come in to administer the epidural, okay? Is someone here with you?"

"My sister," I responded, realizing I was probably gripping her hand too tightly. "Sorry," I said and loosened my grip. "My sister is just parking the car; she'll be back in a couple of minutes."

"Oh, that was nothing!" she said, smiling. "Okay, so your sister will be back…"

"Can I have some water?" I pleaded.

"I'm sorry honey, once you're checked in, we can't give you anything." She paused and looked at me, sympathetically. "How about this? I'll get you a small cup of ice, and you can chew on that for a little bit."

"I'll take whatever I can get, thank you."

"Be right back," she said as she walked out of the room.

Charmaine came in a few minutes later. She pulled a chair close to me and sat down. "Listen, I texted Dylan. He knows now, and I'll keep texting him updates until the baby is born."

"Sounds good."

The nurse walked back in with a few ice cubes in a small paper cup. I grabbed it and started sucking on an ice cube.

It was only about twenty minutes before the doctor came in to examine me, and they wheeled me away in a wheelchair to the L&D area. I gave my sister another copy of the court order. "Could you give this to the nurse in my labor and delivery room?"

"Of course. I'll explain everything; don't worry about a thing. Just focus on your breath."

I was taken into a hallway and was instructed to walk up and down it when Charmaine poked her head in.

"I tracked down the anesthesiologist," she said. "You're next. Let's get you back to the room." I hugged her on the spot.

After the epidural was administered, the doctor helped me lay down. My legs went completely numb. The relief I felt after it kicked in was heavenly. I still felt the tightening in my abdomen, but it no longer felt like each contraction was ripping into my internal organs.

My nurse came in to check my vitals. "You look so relieved," she said with a smile. "Glad they got to you so quickly. My name is Kristie, and I'll be here with you for the next several hours. You can buzz me anytime if you need anything," she pointed to a button on the bed. "Listen, your sister brought me up to speed with everything you've been through. I saw the court order too. I'm so sorry you have to deal with this. I want you to know you're completely safe here... I do have to let you know Dylan was found wandering around on this floor looking for you. Our personnel noticed him immediately, and the police have escorted him to another floor. The police will continue to be around throughout the day. Dylan is not allowed on this floor, and he won't be getting in this room, okay? You are completely safe."

"That guy is a piece of shit," Charmaine said in an annoyed voice. "He *signed* the court order; he *knows* he has to leave you alone." Her face was turning red.

"As long as they keep him out, I'll be all right."

Kristie continued on, holding my chart. "I see you're Dr. MacCabe's patient. Since it's Sunday, she won't be in today. You'll have Dr. Bowman instead. He's a great doctor and will take good care of you. He's the head of the practice."

"Okay, no problem," I told her, though a slight pang of regret ran through me for a minute. I absolutely adored and trusted Dr.

MacCabe and wished I could have held on until tomorrow so she could be there for this. She already knew the heartache I'd been through, and she knew exactly what to say to me to get me in the right frame of mind.

"That's just life, baby," I whispered to my belly, "You're coming just on time."

Dr. Bowman walked in. He was a tall, heavyset man, had a somewhat gruff voice, and seemed very serious – a complete juxtaposition to Dr. MacCabe, the sweet and dainty woman with a hilarious bedside manner.

"How are we doing in here?" he asked me.

"A whole lot better since I got the epidural," I responded.

"At triage, she was 4 cm dilated," Charmaine chimed in.

"Sounds about right," he responded.

As he examined me, he continued talking, "Okay, sweetie, as a reminder, we are a teaching hospital. I'll have a few students coming into and out of the room throughout the day assisting me. Any one of them can help you, but I'm your main guy, okay? Everything looks okay down here, still at 4 cm. You have a long way to go. I'll be back later to check you again."

"Sounds good, doc," I responded.

"I heard about your situation. I'm just confirming; the father will absolutely not be allowed in here, understand? Every staff member on the floor is informed of what's in the court order, and we all are taking this very seriously. Do you have a safe place to stay after you're done at the hospital?"

"I do. I'll be staying at my parents' house. I'll definitely be safe there… Thank you for asking." I was a bit overcome with emotion as I realized how supported I was here.

Charmaine squeezed my hand.

We channel surfed on the television, waiting for me to dilate completely. We found one of the Jason Bourne movies on and left it on that channel for the rest of the day. They were showing the trilogy, as it turned out, so I had something that kept my interest all day. I fell asleep on and off the next few hours, waking up when the contractions got stronger or when one of the doctors or an intern had to check on my progress. Then I'd watch Jason Bourne evading his perpetrators and enjoy the spectacular car chase scenes as Jason maneuvered his way through the streets of Paris at unbelievable speed… until I drifted off to sleep again. I'd look over at Charmaine, who would be checking her phone and dozing off every so often as well.

Ten hours later, it was time. With each push, I gritted my teeth and bore down to get the baby out. I thought I was using everything in me to get him to move. But it didn't seem like the baby was budging at all. About a dozen pushes with all my might, and I was getting nowhere. Nurses, doctors, and interns all were trying to coach me and tell me how to push, what to think about as I pushed, and everyone seemed a bit frustrated at my lack of progress.

"You're going to have to push harder than that, sweetie. Push like you're taking a poop, like *Ummmmm!*," Dr. Bowman said, making a contorted face. I tried not to laugh. *How could he possibly know how hard it was to push a baby out?*

"I'm trying doc; I'm pushing as hard as I can!" I told him.

"Well, to be honest, you're one of the weakest pushers I've ever seen. This baby hasn't moved at all. We'd be done by now if you would just push like you *meant* it."

His comment made me mad enough to spit fire. *Who the hell does he think he is? What an ass!* "I promise you doc; I'm pushing with everything in me. He's not budging!" With the next contraction, I pushed with all the strength I had, so hard that I felt like my eyeballs might pop out. I popped a blood vessel in my eye in the process. Finally, Zach moved down a few centimeters. Just then, the monitors for the baby started beeping incessantly, and a team of nurses rushed in. Dr. Bowman yelled at me, "*Stop* pushing!"

"Oh, for God's sake!" I yelled back.

"Slow down, something's wrong," He looked up at me to explain. "The baby's heart rate slowed down significantly. I know I said you needed to push. Try not to now." As I eased up on the pushing, his heart rate stabilized. Dr. Bowman discovered that my baby was positioned 'sunny side up' in my birth canal. This made it even harder to push the baby out as his head was at an awkward angle, and with every push, that meant his head was being pushed down chin to chest, making an even wider surface area to push down the birth canal.

"We're going to try to ease him out, without dropping his heart rate too low. I want you to listen to me, we'll have to work together, and when I say push, push gently. When I tell you to stop, stop pushing, okay?"

"Okay, I can do that..." I said my head in a full sweat. It felt like 100 degrees in the room.

For the next thirty minutes, there was a push and pull, a stop and start, and Dr. Bowman finally told me he'd be prepping me for a C-Section.

Charmaine jumped into action. "Dr. Bowman, she's not having a C-section. She's almost there - she does not need to be cut open. *Trust me.* I know her better than you do, and believe me when I tell you she is completely capable of having this baby naturally, okay?" She was not taking no for an answer.

He looked at her and shook his head. "I'm going to give her one more shot, and I'm calling it. Vanessa, I want you to give me one more hard push, and we'll see if his head comes out. Are you ready?"

"Ready..."

"Okay, here we go, push!"

"I see his head, Vaness!" Charmaine squealed. "Keep going. His head is almost out!"

"Forceps!" Dr. Bowman demanded. "A couple more pushes, Vanessa, and he'll be all the way out..."

Only a few more pushes and it was over. My baby was born! Dr. Bowman discovered the umbilical cord was wrapped twice around his body, which explained why his heart rate had slowed down every time I'd tried to push.

He showed me my son, the beautiful little baby that had been hiding inside my womb, with the umbilical cord now untangled. He was utterly silent, and his eyes were closed. I couldn't believe that little human had come out of me. I held my breath... *Say something, my little angel! Use your voice!*

Finally, I heard him make his first sounds, crying loudly as he announced himself to the world. It was the most divine, miraculous sound I'd ever heard. The nurses quickly pulled him away to clean him up and weigh him as I waited in the bed, exhausted. I wished like mad that I could stand up and follow the nurses. From the other side of the room, they announced that he was 6 pounds, 7 ounces, and 19 inches long. "He has a fever," I heard someone say.

"Can I hold him?" I pleaded.

"We're just wrapping him up for you, Vanessa," one of the nurses said. After a few seconds, she whisked him over and handed him to me all cleaned up and tightly swaddled, like a perfect little gift. Our eyes locked. His face was tiny, and I didn't know if he could see me very well. I smiled at him. "Hi, Zachary Michael. You've been kicking me like crazy, you little baby," I said to him softly. "I'm your mommy. I love you so much." Tears were streaming down my face. I kissed his little forehead and inhaled his new baby scent. It was divine. Dr. Bowman had pulled him out so carefully with the forceps that there was not a mark on his head to speak of. After what only seemed to be a few seconds, the nurses were pulling him out of my arms, explaining that because he had a fever, he had to go to the NICU. Feeling my face burning up, I knew I, too, had a fever.

I kissed him softly again, barely used to the smell and feel of his fragile skin, and in an instant, he was gone.

I sat there with my sister that evening, feeling eerily empty. Propped up in the hospital bed, the exhaustion I should have been feeling seemed to have disappeared. I was wide awake, trying to understand more about Zachary's condition. My sister reminded me that I needed to eat something. An entire exhausting day had gone by, and I had consumed nothing. It was already past 9 pm by the time I got situated in the recovery room, and the hospital cafeteria was closed. The nurses gave me a few crackers and some ice water, but after the day I'd been through, it just seemed to make me hungrier. Charmaine called Lance, and within the hour, he drove over to see us and brought us some burgers. I counted the minutes until I saw my baby again. Three or four hours later, they returned him.

I had a new nurse this time, named Ally. "Your baby boy is so perfect," she cooed at him before handing him back to me. "I'll be checking your vitals again. We can do this while you're holding the baby, it's no problem." She sat down next to me. "So, I wanted to tell you... the baby's father tried to come to visit Zachary tonight. We didn't let him in."

I kept my eyes on my baby. "How come?" I asked quizzically.

"Well, it was after hours. Visiting time was over. And to be honest, he smelled like alcohol, and he was raising his voice at us... He didn't seem to be in the right state of mind. We'll be better equipped for him to visit in the morning."

I bit my lip. "He was drunk?" I hadn't known Dylan to be a drinker either.

"Well, I don't know if he was drunk, but I could smell it," she said. I was dumbfounded, disappointed, and not sure whether to laugh or cry.

"For goodness sake," Charmaine interjected. "He can't hold it together for one day while the baby's being born?" She turned to look at the nurse. "Any chance we can drug test him before he is handed a newborn? *For safety purposes?*"

Ally looked at both of us apologetically. "I wish I could. Believe me, I don't like this either. All we can do is abide by the court order, and unfortunately, that's not in there. What I can promise you is, he'll be supervised, and I will leave notes for the folks that are here in the morning to make sure to keep a close eye on him."

"All right, I guess," Charmaine responded, disappointed.

"I have to believe he won't hurt his son. That's the only thing that keeps me going," I said back to her. "I trust that God will always keep my baby safe. He will always be safe." I tried to believe it with all my heart.

With my sister's help, we'd started a pattern of feeding the baby, changing him, and dozing off for the next few hours. In no time, I could see the sunlight starting to spill into the room from the window. Eventually, a doctor came by to give me some forms to sign, and they had to take the baby away for a few minutes for his circumcision. My sweet little guy had a lot to endure on his first day of life. They returned him crying, but I nursed him, and he calmed down. About mid-day, one of the nurses informed me that Dylan had come for his first visitation of the baby. A nervous knot pulled tightly in my stomach at the thought of being separated from my son. "I'm always with you in your heart," I told my son. "Be strong, baby, and I'll see you soon, my love." My sister kept me company, asking the nurses when to expect the baby back. About an hour later, the nurse brought Zachary back, asked me to feed him, then returned him to Dylan again for another hour of visitation. I took deep breaths trying not to be upset. I was so attached to him that each moment away made me so anxious. After what seemed an eternity, my son was returned to me. We spent the rest of the day in our recovery room, getting used to one another, and learning how to be our own little family.

The next day went by in a similar fashion, and my time in the hospital was coming to an end. My sister eventually had to get back home to her young children, but my parents and my brother and his family came to visit, and so did a few other friends. It was an amazing feeling seeing so many people I loved, holding my baby boy. I smiled at my father, walking around, bouncing the baby, and singing to him. My mother helped me get my bags packed. My parents had arrived with the car seat and stroller, and I buckled Zach in very carefully, struggling a bit with my hands as they were swollen, as was the rest of my body. As I rolled Zachary out of the room, I looked back one last time at the place where my life had changed forever, thanking God for ushering my son into the world safely, in an extraordinary hospital with wonderful people all around me.

My parents went to get the car from the parking lot, each carrying two vases of flowers. And as I sat in the lobby of the hospital waiting for my dad to pull up, I fought off profound feelings of sadness that were suddenly sweeping over me in waves. *Why isn't his daddy here with us? Why don't I have a husband to take us to our home?* And suddenly I was nervous. *Would I possibly be enough for this precious little soul? I had to be.* I saw my dad's silver SUV pull up. As broken as I still felt, I lifted Zachary up in his car seat and took one shaky step forward, and then another, and then another. I set him into the base of the car seat, just as I had practiced many times, and it wouldn't click in. Over and over I tried, my ego about to burst at not being able to accomplish the simplest thing for my son. Finally, a small miracle occurred. It clicked in. "Phew, piece of cake, baby."

When we arrived back at our home in Morton Grove, we were greeted by my beautiful purple safe haven of a bedroom, with a bassinet set up right next to my bed and even more flower deliveries from multiple friends and co-workers.

I promptly got my ass kicked by motherhood. We did not sleep much the first night. Zach was crying nonstop, and I was desperately trying to get him to latch on to get any kind of nourishment in his body. I was learning, and so was he. Zach was so tiny and so hungry. He cried so hard, and in exhaustion, I let him wiggle onto my naked chest. He was trying desperately to nurse but wasn't quite sure how to latch on. Frustrated and exhausted, we both kept falling asleep like this. I'd wake up and keep trying to push my bosom properly into his mouth. It felt so unnatural, but I kept at it. He would cry and suckle, and we'd fall asleep again, a few minutes at a time. I was worried that he was hungry and wondering why my milk hadn't come in yet. Thankfully the next morning, we went to the pediatrician for his first doctor visit. He gave us a sample of formula with a tiny nipple, and the baby drank some. I immediately noticed how relieved he seemed. He had already lost weight, and that was a scary feeling for me. His skin tone was also a bit yellow, and he needed more sunlight and nourishment. As tired as I was, I had to get him fed and out into the light. Perhaps these were the things that pushed me through the exhaustion. When we got home, the crying continued, but we were relieved to have a little backup supplement with the bottle.

Later that evening, I had to meet Dylan at the church, per our parenting and visitation arrangements. My body felt so beaten down. When I looked in the mirror, I saw the ruptured blood vessels in my left eye from all the pushing during labor. Having to get ready and out of the house so soon seemed impossibly cruel, given the state of exhaustion I was in. *I created this circumstance*, I reminded myself, and Dylan was not allowed in my parents' house. *I am not a victim here.* I decided it was a blessing that I had to keep moving. *Maybe being on-the-go like this will keep me from falling into depression.* That would be the silver lining. I took a shower and put on some fresh clothes and my glasses, using all the energy I had to get Zach ready and buckled safely in the car seat. We made our way to St. Martha's, a quick ten-minute drive from our house.

When I pulled up to the rectory, I saw Dylan's car parked just ahead of us. My heart was racing. I hadn't seen him in months. I didn't know whether I should try to remember him fondly or if I should be angry that he caused me so much pain. I felt my body get hot, trying to sort out all the emotions running through me. He hopped out of his car as I finished parking. *God, he looks so thin.* He was wearing a grey hoodie and jeans that seemed too big for him. Though he was a familiar face, he seemed like a stranger, and any attraction I thought I might have had for him had vanished entirely. He smiled at me as he walked towards us, and part of me felt relieved. It didn't look like he was going to pick a fight with me today.

"Hey there," I tried to sound as casual as possible, though my heart was beating out of my chest. I walked around the car to get Zachary. "Congratulations, you're a dad."

"Yeah.... Thanks," he chuckled. "Congratulations to you too. You did a great job." Even his voice sounded foreign; it had been so long. He took the carrier from my hands as I lifted it out of the base, "I got it." He was grinning at the baby excitedly. "Hi, Zach! It's me again, your daddy!" I was comforted seeing Dylan's eyes so lit up over the baby.

As we stood at the front door of the rectory, waiting for Fr. Dennis to open the door, Dylan handed me a potted plant. "I got you this…" he said awkwardly. *No flowers, nothing pretty, just a plain boring plant.* I grabbed it without looking at it.

"Thanks," I said evenly. *I am not going to let him make me upset, not today.*

Fr. Dennis opened the door. "Hello, you three!" he said warmly. "Is this Zachary? He looks perfect! Congratulations to both of you." He turned his body to invite us in, pointing down the hall. "I'll take you to the living room area where you can sit down comfortably on the couch to visit with the baby."

"Thank you, Father, that sounds perfect." I was so grateful he was willing to open up this space for us. Last month he had offered it to me, knowing my parents did not want Dylan setting foot anywhere near their house. I thought it was a perfect solution. I was completely at home at St. Martha's.

For the next hour, Dylan held the baby, cooing at him. He actually looked comfortable with Zach in his arms, which helped me to relax a little. Dylan made small talk with me too, and I gave him details about Zach's eating and sleeping schedule. I excluded any details that might indicate I was having a tough time. *Not his business.* I watched Zach carefully as his father held him. Dylan was a natural with kids. *I guess he's just not a natural as a husband.* The thought made my heart sink. *I should have figured this out years ago.*

"You look pretty comfortable. I'm just going to close my eyes for a few minutes."

"Totally fine, take a nap," he said as he walked Zachary around the room in his arms. *Might as well take advantage while I can,* I thought. I closed my eyes lightly, still listening to him talking to the baby. After a few minutes, Zachary started crying.

"He's hungry," I announced, and I grabbed a nursing cover walking over to Dylan to take the baby from him. After nursing the baby, I gave him back to Dylan and started to pack up our things to go home.

There were so many things left unsaid that evening, but it was otherwise a perfectly cordial interaction.

"You did a great job, baby boy!" I said to Zach on the drive home. "I hope you enjoyed seeing your daddy." He had already fallen asleep before we arrived home. I looked at him lovingly as I pulled him out of the car and walked him in his car seat back upstairs to our bedroom. *Looks wonderful to be sleeping so peacefully. Maybe I can catch a little nap before he wakes up...*

But it was too late, he was up again, cranky, and hungry again. Zach and I didn't sleep much that second night either. There was a constant changing of diapers, incessant crying, and many, many failed attempts at breastfeeding.

The next day, I found the number of a lactation consultant and made a same-day appointment. After a few days of successful breastfeeding, we finally started to find our rhythm. Meeting with Dylan every few days became no big deal. There were still sleepless nights, but I felt equipped for them, and routines started to kick in.

On the third visit with Dylan, I finally started to skip past the pleasantries… "So, I heard you had a hard time on the night Zachary was born. The nurses told me you'd been drinking and were raising your voice at them, so they didn't let you in?"

He went on the defensive immediately. "Oh my god, that's not what happened at all. I had one beer, and I just wanted to see him for a few minutes. Whatever, it's not worth rehashing." He went silent quickly, his cheeks turning red.

"Okay, well, I'm glad you saw him the very next day, and that you're here with him now. I think it's been working out well. I just wanted to know, for sanity's sake. Are you using any drugs? I wouldn't care if not for the baby."

"No, and I never was! I mean, I've always done pot, and you *knew* that!"

His sense of reality and mine were polar opposites. I snapped back.

"No, I never knew you were a pothead, you failed to mention that during all of our marriage."

"Whatever, you *knew*." I was dumbfounded.

"Well, what about this pink rock I found in your pocket? I did some research of my own, and it was the spitting image of crystal meth. Have you done meth?"

He muttered under his breath. "Oh my god, are you insane? That rock you found wasn't even mine. It was Jessica's. Well, she gave it to me, but I never used it. Her dad made it."

I felt like I was swimming around in a pool of deceit again. "So. Are you telling me Jessica's dad is a meth dealer? It sounds like you picked a winner. She sounds like the perfect mistress. Her husband told me all about her."

He looked exasperated. "NO! It's all marijuana, okay? Her dad made it for me. "And, for the record, I did NOT have an affair! I was with her while we were *separated*, so it doesn't count!"

"Oh my God, are you kidding me?" I raised my voice. "You're so full of shit. I can barely stand it."

"Please be quiet. We are in *church*!"

The fact that he was trying to hush me was laughable. I snorted. "Well, this all sounds ridiculous. So, there are pink rocks that resemble meth but are really marijuana candy, and you get them from your girlfriend's dad. Also, I can barely understand you with all the mumbling you're doing. Can you try to annunciate when you speak to me?" I felt like I was talking to a troubled teenager.

Putting Zach down for bed that night, my blood still boiling, I went back to my pile of books, in desperate search of an answer for what to do with all this anger. *Deep breaths. There's a lesson to be learned here — a silver lining. I just need to remind myself what that is.* I'd figured myself out a lot more over the past few months. There were a series of moments when I'd reflect upon how I was feeling, instinctively pick up one of my books and turn it to a random page, only to discover it was exactly what I needed to read at that time. I started calling it 'divine intervention.' Throughout that process, I stumbled upon many epiphanies for myself, one of which was that my anger was really coming from a place of disappointment and, ultimately, sadness. As I'd been keeping a running list in my journal of quotes that truly resonated with me, there were the two I jotted down that evening that helped me reframe my current state, enough at least to find peace for the evening and fall asleep.

"*You have got to let go of the life you have planned to live the life that is waiting for you.*" – Joseph Campbell

"*The important thing is to be able at any moment to sacrifice what you are for what you can become.*" – Charles Dubios

I decided to use these as a reminder to myself that no matter how upset I felt emotionally, I was ultimately reaching for a greater life than I knew possible. In letting go of the old definition of me – the one attached to any ill feelings toward Dylan – I'd create the best life for my son and myself. As a result, I would be my own hero. That night, I decided wholeheartedly to embrace the lesson and the journey, as hard as it would be the next few months. *I will not sink down; I will rise up. There is no other option.*

Chapter 9: City Lights

My heart raced as I dialed the phone number I'd received a week ago. It was finally time. Miraculously, Zachary had just fallen asleep in his crib moments prior, and I'd tiptoed out of his room and to my office. I looked at my watch — 12:59 pm. I sat waiting, fully attentive at my desk with my journal open in case I needed to take notes.

"Hello, is this Vanessa?" I heard on the other end. Her voice sounded friendly and knowing.

"Hello, Peggy, yes it's Vanessa…"

It had been over a month since Zachary was born. I hadn't been sleeping well, and the strain of being a new mother had thrown my spirit into a setback. Self-doubt had wiggled its way back in. Visitations at St. Martha's rectory vacillated between amicable and contentious, as we tried to find our way as co–parents. A few times, we'd started shouting at one another, disagreeing about the facts around secondhand smoke and the smell of his car. I hated the fight. But my instinct to make Zachary's environment perfect pushed me forward. Deep down, I knew I was reaching for something greater, but it felt *so damn hard*. I was exhausted. I was human. I felt myself withdrawing from regular conversations when I'd be out with Zachary. *Why did it seem everyone always zeroed in on me, asking about the baby's father?* I was a single mom. I couldn't shake off the shame of it.

Peggy Rometo was a well-known intuitive reader whom I'd stumbled upon one afternoon as I was listening to Hay House Radio, a talk radio station with various show hosts who discussed a range of topics from psychology to relationships to emotional support to intuition. Exasperated by my setbacks, and feeling stuck with my emotional baggage, I went online and scheduled an appointment with Peggy after listening to one of her talk shows. Her persona had intrigued me from the beginning of the show; she seemed to cut right to the truth in relationships. Her advice was honest and practical. I wanted so badly for someone to throw me some breadcrumbs to help me find my way.

"Okay, Vanessa, what I'll do now is breathe and connect to our message, and we'll go from there." She spoke quickly, almost urgently. She paused to breathe, and there were a few seconds of silence. "Please know, Vanessa, you need to continue to release insecurity, fear, and doubt. Know that as you settle into a more comfortable position, it is important for you to continue to release pain and suffering and prepare for the upcoming storm. It is important during this time that you not sequester yourself and learn to rely on others who care, who do not make you feel that you are a burden. They're showing me this space of movement... I see you sitting around with all these boxes of your stuff around you and feeling this sense of enormity. There's this feeling of *What am I going to do?*" Her accuracy was jaw-dropping. I looked around my office wide-eyed, noticing half of it was stacked with boxes that I had yet to unpack.

"Wow, it's uncanny. I am literally sitting in a room with boxes full of my things. I am going through a divorce, and I just had our baby about a month ago. I moved in with my parents, and I'm raising this little boy. It's been shocking and happened so quickly. It's been the hardest time of my life..."

"Awww… I'm so sorry. I'm sure you have questions. How can I help you today?"

I'd prepared for this. "I really just want to know what the best way is for me to heal. How long will it be before I start to feel better? How do I get through this and make things as best as they can be for myself and my baby?"

She paused again for a breath. "This ongoing process is happening to awaken you, to find newfound stability, and to find comfort in your own skin. This time is about finding a resilience that you didn't know you had. My sense is, you're already doing great considering what the heck you've just gone through. You're starting to realize that you're stronger than you ever knew. This time is about an awakening to what you want, what your desires are, and what you want to create in your life for yourself and your son. This is about creating a new relationship with your ex-husband. As he matures and you keep standing up for yourself, the results will be in your highest good. This is a whole new level of shock, what he's pulled here on you. But, slowly over time, he'll pull back towards the person you once knew… There's this whimsical energy about him. It's like he can be really intense or passionate when he talks about a subject, but then there's a wind underneath him, and then he just leaves. It's like two opposite energies in him." I was so shocked by her accuracy that I accidentally dropped my notebook on the floor.

"Wow, Peggy, you're completely right about his personality," I said, leaning over to pick up my notebook, "and I wish I didn't have to deal with him. Day to day, this divorce has been a roller coaster for me. Yesterday I felt decent, and the day before, I went to church and cried for hours. I'm tired of the fighting and the anxiety. The battles between our attorneys are getting us nowhere. There's so much to sort out with the parenting schedule, our finances, our condo… I have started to wonder if we should just go through a mediator…"

The ongoing battle between us was truly taking a toll on my emotional well-being. One night, in particular, my rage came to a boiling point. Seeing Dylan at St. Martha's for his regular Thursday night visit with Zach, he told me that he was coming after me for alimony, to offset anything that he should have to pay for child support. "I make less money than you because you didn't give me a chance to go to grad school, so it's really you at fault that I'm in this financial situation," he explained to me coldly.

"Do you mean to tell me you don't think you should have to pay any child support? Do you seriously think that your son isn't your financial responsibility?" I could feel my cheeks getting hot.

"I'm telling you that you should pay me alimony because I sacrificed going to grad school for you, and now you make more money than me."

I could barely even speak. "When the hell did you ever want to go to grad school? And now you want a *payout* for that? Do you want to pay off my student loans, then?"

"No! I just want what's fair, and I think it's fair that the alimony and child support cancel each other out."

In my entire life, I don't recall being as angry as I was at that moment. *What a fucking piece of work he is!* Getting home was a blur. My heart was racing, and I could feel myself losing control of my emotions as I pulled into the driveway. *How can he have such little regard for financial responsibility when it comes to his own son? It's not even about the amount of money; it's about the ownership of his son's well-being. Where is that, if he's only playing tit for tat with his theoretical grad school option? He never once showed real interest in going back to school!* I walked back into my parents' house, holding the baby, and my entire body was shaking. I noticed Charmaine had come over, though I could barely see through the hot tears streaming out of my eyes. She ran over as soon as she saw my face.

"Please hold him," I urged her. "I just need a few minutes to myself. I'm so angry I can't talk about it..."

"Oh my God, what's wrong?" my mom asked. She and my father had walked over to us, with serious concern coming over their faces.

"Just let her be," Charmaine interjected. She turned back to me, "Go out to the car, Vaness... Please don't drive anywhere this upset, though." She'd pulled the baby out of his car seat and began rocking back and forth, holding him. It was too cold outside to take a walk. And she was right; I was no longer in the right frame of mind to be driving. I ran back out to the car and slammed the door shut. With my blood boiling over, I did the only thing I could think of doing, which was screaming at the top of my lungs while punching my hands on the steering wheel until my throat literally went raw. *Could he possibly win in court with this logic? Am I crazy? How the hell did I get into this situation? God, what did I do so bad to deserve this?* After screaming every profanity I could possibly think of at my windshield, all my energy was zapped. There were no more tears left in me. I sat there for a few more minutes doing some deep breathing. When I opened my eyes, I was staring down the street where I'd grown up. I remembered taking a big fall off of my bike one afternoon when my dad had the rare chance to take me for a ride. As I fell on the curb scraping my knee pretty badly, my eyes welled up with tears, ready to lose it. It was one of my only chances to spend time like this with my dad, and I'd messed it up. Suddenly he picked me up off the ground, brushing off my knee with his hand. He put me back on the bike. "Just keep going," he said stoically. He turned back to his bike and kept riding. I forgot about my fall, pedaling hard to keep up with him. It was my first lesson in resilience.

In the quiet of my own breath, I suddenly became so peaceful that I could have fallen asleep if it hadn't been for my sister knocking on the window.

"Hey, Vaness…. I have to go home. Mom's holding the baby, and I think he's getting hungry."

"Okay, thanks. I'll head in now." *Time to pick myself up. If this is rock bottom for me, then it's the perfect place to bounce back. There's a baby counting on me to be a better person.* I hugged her before I walked into the house. "Love you, Char."

"Feeling better, baby?" my dad asked as I closed the front door. He walked over to the foyer and put his arm around me comfortingly.

"Yes, dad, thanks," I said. I gave him a big hug. "Gotta just keep going."

Peggy paused as if listening to an answer she was downloading… "Please know, Vanessa, you need to learn to trust your instincts. If you do go forward with a mediator, it feels like there will be more honesty, and you'll make progress faster. In general, it feels better for Zachary to see his father. While Dylan deeply hurt you, there's a part of you that very much cares for him and wants him to have a second chance to believe in him to do the right things. But it is good that the mama bear in you is standing up and saying *hey, this is what it has to look like.*" Though my ego wanted to protest the part about believing in him, I knew she was right. Loving someone doesn't turn off like a light switch. The truth was, I wanted him to succeed at being a father, even if he had failed me as a partner.

"Can Dylan be trusted to care for a newborn baby by himself? I'm worried about him being on drugs."

"You're being asked to table your logic in some of the behavior you've seen from him... to know that Zachary will be better off with a relationship with his father. There's no benefit to you for your son to hate him. You're learning a lesson in unconditional love. Know your son is protected by love." I sighed. It wasn't a direct answer to whether or not he was responsible. I had to trust in Dylan's love for our son, and that had to be enough.

Peggy continued talking about various aspects of the divorce, asking me to release any nervous energy around it, and not to feel threatened. "My sense is that you're going to be just fine. Is there anything else you'd like to ask?"

I paused, almost afraid to ask the question on my mind. *Maybe this is silly.* I spit it out anyway. "Well... I do... I wonder about finding love again. I know I'll find my true partner someday. What's he like?" I was so impressed by the accuracy of what she could see in my present situation that I decided to ask her about my future.

"Of course, yes..." she paused again. "Open-hearted, warm, he's really a family man, devout in his faith. There's real spiritual energy inside of him that surprises you, because externally he's a good-looking guy, and you don't expect him to have such a Christian heart. You'll have a lot of fun together too. He's an entrepreneur, really smart. It seems like he's a professional guy in construction or something like that. I see a lot of kids around you in the future, so you're either having more kids, or he'll have kids from a previous relationship… Here's the thing, it won't be very long before you meet him. You won't miss him. He won't *let* himself be missed. It's like a *whirlwind*. It's shocking, powerful, a strong pull that you've never had before."

"Wow, that all sounds great," I chuckled. "Sounds like I'm in for a really bright future." I was reminded of the dream I'd had not too long ago, lying next to my partner in the grass on the 4th of July. Even through all my heartbreak, something inside me never let go of the dream of having a fantastic love story. Years ago, I'd had a private consultation with Sonia Choquette, who suggested to me that the reason I loved photographing weddings was because I was studying love, trying to understand it and experience it myself. Happily married at the time, I'd filtered out what she said and had forgotten about it.

Peggy ended the session by helping me to visualize the energy of healing and protection surrounding me.

For the past few months, I'd also started seeing a new therapist named Joan. She had a different, more 'text-book' approach that I appreciated thoroughly. In our next session, Joan instructed me to write down some of my 'automatic thoughts' that had been keeping me up at night on notecards. On the backside of each notecard, I was to write down statements refuting these thoughts with logical explanations and evidence. I started off with my first automatic thought, and probably the one that had consumed me the most lately:

I am an idiot for not knowing he did not love me.

Joan and I spent a lot of time on this one. It took quite a bit of convincing on her part to remind me that I really wasn't an idiot, that I had to be kinder with my own thoughts about myself. Finally, we settled on the refuting statements:

I am not an idiot; I am just guilty of trusting my husband, who I thought was faithful. I am not an idiot because he was good at hiding his feelings. I am not an idiot. He is just a confused individual who probably doesn't know how he feels.

On a second card I wrote my next automatic thought:

There must be something wrong with me.

And on the reverse side I wrote:

There's nothing wrong with me. I'm not broken. I'm just getting out of a bad relationship.

Now getting the hang of it, I wrote a third one:

My holidays without my son will be devastating.

On the flipside I wrote:

It may be hard at first, but I will get accustomed to the schedule. Many people go through a divorce with children involved and still enjoy holidays. I will too.

It was a technique to rewire my brain – to automatically change the channel out of a fear-based mentality and into one that was more balanced and trusting. I loved Joan's approach. I carried those notecards around with me like a safety blanket for the next few weeks, and whenever the fear started to creep in, I'd pick the card tied to that fear and read the refuting evidence. Surprisingly, it actually worked. The exercise coincided directly with something I'd read by Wayne Dyer, where he mentioned: "When you change the way you look at things, the things you look at change."

As we approached October, my routine with Zach was getting more comfortable. In the evenings, I would bathe him and then nurse him until he fell asleep, usually at 9 pm on the dot. He was just starting to babble, and a few times I was sure I heard him say, *mama*. I was so in love with this boy. I'd talk to him about our home and our future, and I'd promise him, no matter what, we'd be happy together. He would coo at me and smile, and I started to realize that we were already as happy as we ever needed to be. In those moments, I felt like the luckiest mom in the world. He was sleeping in his crib now, and I would have quiet time for myself to read and journal, an essential part of who I now was. I started to daydream about what our life would be like in a few years. In my heart, I wanted to find new love, for him and for me. I wanted a father for my son, and while I knew he had a father in Dylan, what I wanted more than anything was a tight family unit, a force in our lives who would love both of us unconditionally. It was such a strong desire I could feel it emanating from my pores.

My ego told me I'd need more time because I wasn't nearly through the divorce process yet and that I'd probably have to be alone for many years. *You have baggage. You're going through a divorce and have a baby you're raising. Who would sign up for that?* I did my best to put those thoughts aside and just write down what it would *feel* like to have new love, to be indeed seen and appreciated for who I am, and to receive from a man in a way I never had before. Journaling about it was like treating myself to a mental vacation, imagining this incredible man, and everything he would be for us.

To the love of my life,

I want to thank you in advance for finding me. For finding us. I've always known you were out there, searching for us. I love the father you've become to my son, how you took him in as your own without any hesitation. You've taken us into your life as a package deal, and we fit into your life seamlessly. Your eyes are genuine, and so is your heart. I love how brilliant you are at business, the way you handle yourself in a room, taking charge of things. There's a confidence in you that I learn from every day. You make me better, just by being yourself. Thank you for seeing who I really am and loving every part of it. Being a mother has become even more enjoyable with you as my partner in this life. I love how you kiss my forehead, how you pull me close at our favorite Latin restaurant. I can't believe how much we have in common, and yet we're different enough to learn from one another constantly. You are about as picky as they get, and you knew exactly what you were looking for. It might have taken you a while to find me; sorry about that. I promise, I was getting myself ready, so I'd come with no strings attached. I'm learning to stand on my own two feet, and I'm falling in love with life first. When we finally do meet, it will feel like a key and lock have finally found their match. This is the magic of life at its finest. Thank you for everything you are. I love you with all my heart. I can't wait to meet you.

I went back to work at the end of October. My good friend Cathy had offered to nanny for Zach, and it was ideal to have someone I completely trusted to help me through the transition. We'd been good friends since we were little girls, living only a block apart for most of our adolescence. Before Cathy started, she made a point to come over to the house, and together we organized everything to make it as easy as possible for her to take over for me. We made a great team. All of Zach's bottles were freshly sanitized and lined up perfectly, we set a schedule for his feedings and naps, and diapers and wipes were stocked at his changing table. I packed my work bag with my laptop, a fresh notebook for work, my journal, and my rosary.

"You got this girl!" Cathy told me as I put my backpack on and turned to leave.

"Thanks, Cathy, I hope so!"

"Call me whenever you want, and if you want to FaceTime at any time during the day, we can. Don't forget your breast pump!" She handed me the black Medela bag that carried my pump and all the accessories that went along with it. Being a working mom who was still lactating was going to be quite an effort.

"Thanks, girl. You're the best!" I put my arm around her to squeeze her while she was holding the baby. "Bye, my little bubba..." I kissed Zach on his cheek and held back some bittersweet tears. I was ready for life to carry on.

It was a crisp fall day as I hopped on the train downtown. I felt so much lighter riding the train alone, no longer burdened by twenty-five pounds of extra body weight and a baby moving in my belly. I'd already gotten back down to my original pre-pregnancy size, and though my shape wasn't exactly the same, I fit my work clothes comfortably. I gazed up in awe of the tall buildings just outside of Union Station. It was like seeing Chicago for the first time. I felt a buzz in the air as hundreds of people emerged from underground, marching off to their jobs in their business attire and walking with such purpose. I smiled, looking up that the building I'd worked in for so many years — my old stomping grounds. I imagined someday being immersed in the thick of it again, having dinner at a hip new restaurant with some friends. *Someday.*

It was a warm welcome back at the office. I spent most of the morning saying hello to all my colleagues and culling through hundreds of emails. Before I knew it, I was back home in Morton Grove, reunited with my son. The smile on his face the moment he saw me always seemed to take my breath away. I loved his boy more than life itself.

The more consuming parts of my life at this point were the sessions with our mediator, Marjorie, who was helping us plow through the bits and bytes of our divorce agreement. Every other Thursday evening, we had a two-hour mediation session in Northbrook, a suburb north of Morton Grove. I'd usually bring the baby along with me at the sessions.

One evening in the middle of our mediation session, Dylan, who was holding the baby in his arms for the past hour, leaned over and said, "I think he pooped. Can you give me a diaper and some wipes?" I handed him my diaper bag and watched him set the changing pad on top of the conference room table we were sitting at and lay the baby down on it. He was about to change the poopy diaper right here in front of Marjorie, instead of using the bathroom. He pulled off the baby's pants and started to undo the onesie he was wearing.

"Um…. Is this okay?" I asked apologetically. I stood up and got ready to assist. Zach had had some diarrhea lately, and I was wary of what he'd reveal once he took the diaper off.

"Well... okay, it's fine..." I sensed some hesitation in Marjorie's voice. "Hopefully, it's not a big mess..." Dylan was moving quickly, taking charge without noticing that Marjorie and I were not exactly comfortable with this setup.

"Crap!" I heard Dylan say. I looked over at him, and somehow, he'd gotten the baby's liquid poop smeared across his shirt. It was a mess. But it wasn't nearly as bad as the smell.

"Shoot!" I grabbed some wipes and threw them at Dylan so he could clean his shirt and pulled the baby towards myself with another fist full of wipes. Luckily, I'd had a few gallon-sized Ziploc bags in my diaper bag, and I started throwing all the poopy wipes into one of them, trying to move as fast as I could. As I got the last of the poop wiped off of his butt and the changing pad, I reached for a diaper. I noticed my shirt felt wet. Zach was peeing on me, and it was getting all over the table. "Shoot, shoot, shoot!" I squealed as I grabbed anything I could find in the diaper bag. I found Zach's baby blanket and threw it over at Dylan. "Wipe the table!" Dylan got to work on the table while I fastened the diaper onto Zach as quickly as I could, picking him up in one arm while wiping my shirt with another. Dylan grabbed the baby's clothes and tried to help me get them back on him. As I stood there watching Dylan fumble around with the snaps of the onesie, I started laughing.

"Well, you smell like shit," I nudged him with my elbow chuckling.

"And you smell like piss!" he responded. We started laughing so hard I had to wipe tears out of my eyes.

After we finished our laughing fit, Marjorie looked at us like she was looking at two young kids. "It looks like you two are learning how to co-parent." She beamed at us. "You make a decent team, don't you think?"

The lessons I'd learned from the many months of self-examination had brought me to new realizations that I was now starting to accept. I started seeing Dylan through a new lens, one that felt compassionate, and I understood that he, too, was hurting in his own way over this divorce. I stopped seeing him as an enemy that needed to be defeated, and instead as a person who was far from perfect and was, like me, trying to find his way. While I didn't exactly feel like being his best friend, the fact that I could acknowledge this new way of seeing him was a significant breakthrough for me.

The reality was: neither Dylan nor I knew what the hell we were doing in this ongoing battle, fighting solely from a place of ego where we were trying to "win" for fear of "losing out" on something. Neither of us had been through a divorce, and neither of us knew what it would be like to share a schedule with a baby when we were no longer a couple. I'd been stuck in fear, worried about every weekend and holiday with my baby as if my life depended on it. With the finalization of the divorce on the horizon, I had to dig even deeper as the reality of not having my son every single night started to sink in. With Marjorie's guidance, we made progress, some days more than others, but we had indeed turned a corner on how this co-parenting agreement could work.

In November, I did a search on meetup.com and found a group called "Women in their Thirties Going Through Separation or Divorce." I was surprised that such a specific group existed, but that was just one of the many magical things about Chicago. You could find literally anything you could imagine if you looked hard enough. It was time for me to stop living with my nose in a book and start connecting with the outside world again. After chatting with some of the members of the group, we decided to meet for dinner downtown on a Saturday night. My parents agreed to watch the baby for the evening, and I was excited! I searched my closet for a completely different set of clothes – my "going out" clothes. I found a pair of jeans that fit me just right, and a cute body-hugging floral V-neck top with three quarter length sleeves. I dressed it up with a pair of black heels and carefully put on my makeup, going heavier on this than I'd done in a long, long time. I relished the drive downtown and couldn't help but smile as I drove towards that beautiful skyline. *Someday is today.*

We met at a popular Italian restaurant downtown called Centro. It was oddly warm outside, considering it was mid-November. After chatting in the lobby of the restaurant for a few minutes, we all decided it was nice enough for us to sit outside. There were 10 of us, and I was comforted seeing women my age actively seeking support from other women in the process of divorce. We all took a turn at the table, sharing a two-minute snapshot of our stories, and it blew my mind. As it turned out, I wasn't a freak that couldn't be related to. There was a gorgeous red-headed woman named Jane, whose ex ended up being an abusive drunk, and they were in the final stages of their divorce. There was Elaina, a beautiful Latina woman with a five-year-old daughter, whose husband had turned out to be gay. There was Charlotte, the therapist, whose husband had cheated on her. There was Paula, the graphic designer, who felt like she'd just lost her best friend. There was Abby, the single mom to a four-year-old boy, whose ex-husband had moved away and left her with no money or support.

"Wow, I honestly didn't know how many painful stories there were out there," I said, sipping a glass of wine after sharing my own personal story. "I thought I was alone in this, like some kind of freak. Thank you for showing me I'm not. Cheers to all of you for being survivors."

"You're definitely not a freak, Vanessa," Jane assured me as she raised her glass to me, and we toasted. These women understood me, understood the pain of rejection and the profound sadness of feeling unloved. And before I knew it, I was a sharing more about my experiences, along with some helpful insights I'd gleaned while I'd read myself into oblivion the past few months at home.

The mere existence of such a support group was a small miracle to me. Suddenly, I had soul sisters who walked a similar path. I went out one night to sing karaoke with Elaina for her birthday. I took Zach on his first downtown outing to the Chriskindlmarket, meeting up with some girlfriends for lunch and enjoying the beautiful downtown Christmas lights. I was too busy setting up plans to sit and ponder the divorce for too long. As the weeks wore on, my Spirit started to reboot. A new me was emerging, one that worried less and enjoyed life more.

Chapter 10: The Secret

As if my Spirit knew I was entering the next chapter of my life, just before Christmas, I had another vivid dream.

As twilight turned to dawn, the winding road I'd been driving down led me to a small town. Cabins lined the streets and I let myself wander around, turning and turning through the neighborhood in my pickup truck, getting my bearings. Though I wasn't completely comfortable, I was intrigued by the simplicity and beauty of the town. I noticed I was now alone in the truck, but I wasn't afraid. The sun was just starting to peek through the tops of the mountain that seemed to frame this village, casting a pink haze over antique stores, candy shops, clothing retailers, and other quaint markets. My eyes lit up thinking about how fun it would be to browse through the shops once they opened up.

I noticed a side road at the end of the street, and I urged myself onward, suddenly remembering that I had an appointment I didn't want to be late for. I knew I was close. The side road started winding through a lush green forest. I was approaching a large log cabin. A man was sitting outside of it tending to a fire. It was Angel. He waved me closer. Pulling the pickup truck to the side of the road, I climbed out and walked towards him, smiling. "Hey! I thought I lost you."

"Never," he said with his eyes, the reflection of the sun rising in the sky creating a twinkle in his eye. He placed his hand on my back and led me to the front door of the cabin. I knocked on the door. Before I could finish knocking, it started to open.

Sonia, now wearing beautiful green and purple scarf and a casual t-shirt and jeans, welcomed me inside with a smile. "You're just in time! Follow me." The cabin looked much larger inside than it did from the outside. We walked through a spacious living room with a large oriental area rug sprawled across the wooden floor with a brown leather couch on one end and some throw pillows spread around the rug in front of the fireplace. She motioned over to a ladder that led to a loft area inside the cabin. There was a large window up top that had an absolutely stunning view of the mountains as well as the small lake located just beyond the main street. There was a long, deep beautifully upholstered bench at the base of the window where we both sat cross legged, facing each other. The light of the morning streamed in and I sat in wonder, feeling like an important secret was about to be shared with me. "I know you've been worried, but I wanted you to remember that everything is working out for you. Trust in that. Close your eyes and take a breath with me."

I did as she said, closing my eyes and inhaling deeply. There was a soft, milky sandalwood scent in the air that made me feel instantly present with my own Spirit. At the same time, I fought with the thoughts in my head as I tried to sustain this state of peace. We sat there in silence for a few minutes, and I refocused, listening to the sound of my own breath.

When I finally opened my eyes, she returned my gaze and said, "I have proof. There's something I want to show you." She reached down into her purse that had been on the floor next to us and pulled out three photos. She placed all of them in front of me neatly in a row from top to bottom. They were black and white, grainy images that I couldn't decipher. I cocked my head to one side, curious.

"I don't understand what this is, Sonia."

"Maybe not yet. Just trust it." She quickly changed the subject. "My daughters are almost here, so I have to get going." She got up quickly and climbed down the ladder.

I woke up the next morning curious about what I'd been shown in my dream, but by the sound of Zach's crying I knew he was hungry. I got up to start my day, quickly pushing the dream from my mind.

Chapter 11: Calling In "The One" ™

Putting up the Christmas decorations felt extra special this year. We hung ornaments and lights on the Christmas tree and wrapped the staircase banisters with a festive garland. We also hung up a Filipino lantern, called a *parol*. It was a beautiful star-shaped, multi-colored glass lantern with multiple bulbs inside that flickered in a pattern. We hung it in the window at the top of the staircase, overlooking the walkway. Zach was almost six months old. He was fascinated by all the holiday lighting in the house, and I spent each evening walking him around the house to admire our work.

For Christmas dinner, I dressed the baby in a festive red sweater and jeans. I'd also bought myself a new outfit: a black and tan lace blouse, which I layered with a black cardigan, black leggings, and black leather boots. I felt pretty. I was comfortable in my body again.

Before we ate, we all stood behind our seats at the table and said grace, my mother reading a set of prayers from a pamphlet she had printed out earlier that day. I kept my eyes closed as I listened to her voice, fervently thanking God for the miracle of my son, and for the blessing we had to spend our very first Christmas Eve with each other. Tomorrow, I'd have to hand him off to Dylan, and I was already feeling the pangs of separation. I wanted to make tonight count. By now, Zach was old enough to enjoy some solid food, and he was happily sucking on mashed potatoes and smiling unabashedly at all seven of his smitten cousins who were taking turns cooing at him and holding his little feet.

Before we opened presents, we took photos in front of the tree. Determined not to let my photography skills go to waste, I took the pictures of David's and Charmaine's family and finally handed Charmaine my camera to take some photos of Zach and me. This year instead of Dylan, I had my sweet baby as my partner, and I held him proudly. We stayed up late, I drank wine with my brother and sister, and soon Zach was dozing off in my arms. Wishing I could make the time last longer, and I snapped a few selfies of us on my phone just before I set him into his crib for the evening.

"Merry Christmas, my sweet," I whispered as I kissed both his cheeks.

"What's the plan for tomorrow, Vaness?" Charmaine asked as I emerged from Zach's bedroom.

"We're going to the 11 am Mass, and Dylan's picking him up afterward. Are you going to church with us?" We made plans to go to mass and lunch the following day.

Sharing my baby on the holidays was a tough pill for me to swallow. I knew it was the right thing to do, but it still hurt to give him up. After church the next morning, I went outside to the parking lot at St. Martha's and saw Dylan in his car, eagerly awaiting his turn with the baby. I saw genuine excitement in his face, and I was consoled knowing that my baby was going to be absolutely adored all day. That gave me enough strength to say goodbye. I watched them drive away with a smile on my face, but as the car disappeared down the street, it suddenly felt like Christmas was over, a pang of loneliness pressing on my heart. Empty-handed, I stuffed my hands into my coat pockets and walked back into the church. I distracted myself by talking to fellow parishioners, wishing everyone a Merry Christmas. I barely knew what to do with my arms when I wasn't holding the baby. Looking over at Charmaine and Lance, who were talking to some friends, I noticed Liam was now awake from his nap and was smiling at me from his stroller. I picked him up and kissed him on the cheek.

"Will you be my baby for today?" I asked him as he giggled.

Arriving home later that afternoon, I grabbed my iPad and threw myself onto my bed, laying on my belly, and pulled up an article that I'd read the previous week. It was a story about being a single mom and having to share the kids. The author explained what her first days without her children felt like. It was as if her reason for being ceased to exist when they were gone. The house was so quiet, she continuously checked their rooms 'just in case' she'd lost her mind, and they were actually home. I could relate. My phone buzzed, and I reached down to the floor and grabbed it from out of my purse. It was a message from Stella, Dylan's grandmother.

Hi Vanessa! I'm having a great time with my great-grandson. He looks so cute in the sweater I knitted him for Christmas! I miss you, and you'll always be my granddaughter, no matter what happened. Merry Christmas, and I love you!

She attached a photo of her holding my son, and my heart melted. I wiped a few tears out of my eyes. Zach was perfectly safe and sound and was surrounded by people who loved him. That was all I could ever possibly want for him.

Sitting up, I decided to grab my journal from my nightstand, and without stopping to think, I wrote at the top of the page:

Everything I am grateful for in my marriage with Dylan:

I started scribbling whatever came to mind.

- *I have an amazing baby whom I love more and more every minute*

- *Stella, the kindest sweetest soul who will always be a grandmother to me*

- *For being accepted into their family for the past ten years with open arms*

- *For beautiful memories at my in-law's lake house in Indiana…for pontoon boat rides and so many wonderful Fourth of July memories. I know my baby will have many adventures there too, and I'm glad I got to experience them for myself.*

I continued to fill the pages with good memories, and let the bad ones fade out into the background. A rush of energy came through me as I remembered laughing with Dylan's sister over a Pictionary game, and then I remembered the trip we all took to Phoenix, where we rented a small house, and soaked in the outdoor hot tub, admiring the starlit sky at night. As I continued writing, I felt like light was entering into me through my hands and into my heart. Allowing the good times to flow through my being seemed to heal the scars of hurt that still existed inside my energetic body. I smiled as I realized that I was completely fine with these being memories of the past, rather than hopes for the future. The truth was, I was looking forward to what my new life would bring me, and I wondered what it would feel like to someday find the right partner for me and Zach. Sitting on the floor next to my nightstand was a pile of unread books that I still wanted to read, and I zoomed in on one: *Calling In "The One": 7 Weeks to Attract the Love of Your Life* by Katherine Woodward Thomas. I'd added it to my shopping cart months ago, knowing full well I wasn't ready to read it, but wanting to give myself something to look forward to someday. The book seemed to be a step-by-step guide on how to find your true soul mate. *Could it really be as simple as reading this book?* I wondered. The skeptical side of me believed it wasn't possible, but the more dominant, open-hearted side of me believed it really could be that simple, and that anything I set my intentions on, I could manifest into reality. I reached over and picked it up, flipping through some of the pages. I felt the weight of its magic in my hands. It felt right to me. *I'm almost ready to find you, Mr. Wonderful. Almost.* I knew that in order to move forward in this direction though, I needed to operate from a place of wholeness. I didn't need anyone completing me. And the happier I became in the present, the closer I was to being ready to share my life with someone new. Stacking it back on top of the books next to the nightstand, I gave it a little pat at the top of the pile. *I'm coming for you soon.*

Before I knew it, it was time to pick up Zachary again, and when I put him to bed that evening, I fell into the most delicious and peaceful sleep that I'd had in a long time.

In early December, I had discovered a holistic healthcare center in Glenview that was advertising a workshop on starting a new year right. Its focus was on connecting to your inner self and finding true meaning in 2013. It was right up my alley. When I showed up to the workshop on January 2nd, I was surrounded by a new tribe of people that were different than my support group. There were men and women of various ages and backgrounds, about fifteen of us in total. And all of us were eager to step into something new and different this year.

We went around the room to start, and each of us described a little bit of our story, explaining what brought us here and what we hoped to get out of the day. I was floored by the heavy stories people brought with them; mine felt quite small in comparison. One older gentleman was grieving the loss of his wife, who had passed away from cancer years ago. Another woman had lost her son in the military a few years prior, and she had been in a deep depression ever since. I kept it simple. "My husband left me when I was five months pregnant. I'm going through a divorce now, raising a baby who's about six months old, and working my way through the healing process. I'm done being sad, and I want to use today to kick start a happy year for me." The story that once felt so shocking and painful, no longer caused me pain to talk about.

We spent the afternoon cutting photos and images out of magazines and pasting them onto a sheet of cardboard. The instructions were loose – cut out anything that catches your eye or speaks to you. I wasn't sure what the point of the exercise was, but I enjoyed flipping through magazines that were spread out throughout the healing center, looking for things that I liked in the pages. I found a gem of a picture where a boy and girl were running carefree in a field, holding some lightweight fabric that seemed to float as it caught in the wind. I chose it to be the main image in my collage. I found another image of a woman stepping out of the water at a beach, looking strong and magnificent. I also found several scenic photos of beaches and sunsets that had gorgeous blue and purple tones to it and used them to frame my main image. When the exercise was over, the workshop facilitator, Dana, explained, "Imagine, for a moment, that this entire exercise was a way for your Spirit to send you a message. Our Spirits talk to us all the time through imagery and abstracts, similar to when you're dreaming. What we've done this afternoon is allow you to find images that speak to you, through the hundreds of random magazines that were scattered throughout our entire office space. I'd like to suggest that what *you* chose, and what caught *your* eye, actually was not random at all. Let's take the next ten minutes now to really look at that art we've just created and write down the message you think your Spirit has for you. What message did you receive?" *Wow.* I looked at my collage for a moment, closed my eyes, and took a deep breath. A simple phrase came to my mind immediately. "Remember to play." I realized that all this time, I'd been pushing forward so seriously, meticulously trying to unlock the key to healing. I made a vow to myself to let my heart lighten and to do things that would help me to be more carefree.

In the following weeks, I made a conscious effort to do more of what would fill my cup. I signed up Zach for lessons at the local Gymboree so that he could start socializing with other babies, and I could interact with other young moms. I signed up for a local gym membership that included childcare, allowing me some very needed *me-time* without burdening my parents or anyone else to watch the baby for me. And, for the first time since moving out of the city, I got my hair cut. My hair had grown way past my shoulders while I was pregnant, and I missed the short bob that I used to wear. Looking at myself in the mirror after my 'city girl' haircut was back in place, I felt like I was coming back to life.

After I'd put the baby down to bed one night a few weeks later, I grabbed the book at the top of the pile by my nightstand and said, "Okay Vanessa, it's now or never, let's *do* this."

Flipping open to the first page of *Calling in "The One,"* I read the following words:

Be realistic.
Plan for a miracle.
- Bhagwan Shree Rajineesh

Katherine Woodward Thomas prefaced her book with an explanation of her own personal story and how she attracted the right person into her life after several unfulfilling relationships. She changed her own inner dialogue, set an intention for what she wanted, and found the love of her life. She did it so boldly and brilliantly, and it was hard not to ooze with enthusiasm after reading about it. Her book was structured in the style of a seven-week course, with lessons to read each week and exercises to perform as you internalized the lesson of the week. And so, with a heart wide open and ready for the lessons I was about to receive, I began.

Chapter One's exercise started with a yoga-like move of extending arms out first in front of me, and then opening them up to either side, imagining my heart opening up. "I open myself fully to give and receive love," I said out loud. I did this movement several times as the book suggested, and though it felt silly at first, I kept an open mind. There was no turning back now. In genuinely allowing myself to go through the movements and repeat those words to myself, it felt like a literal opening up to the universe and feeling ready for its embrace, and I believed with everything in me that I had opened a portal into a place of magic. I was on my way.

I told no one about this little experiment until the second week. When Cathy arrived on a Monday morning to take care of Zach while I headed out to work, I said with a sly smile on my face, "So, I thought you might be interested to know. I'm almost ready to start dating again."

"Really? Vanessa! I'm so excited for you!" she squealed. "I've been wondering if you were ready. You seem so happy lately. I've been telling Tine it's time for you to find a real man." Tine was her husband and college sweetheart.

"Thanks! I really am happy again. I think dating sounds like a fun idea, though I have no idea what I'm doing! I started reading this book…" I explained what it was about, and her eyes lit up with excitement.

"Seven weeks? That sounds awesome! I have a feeling you're going to kill this like you do everything else you set your mind to!" I gave her a quick hug and ran off to start the day. I had a big smile on my face as I sat on the train, reading the next pages of the book. *Okay, Universe, I'm ready for the magic, bring it on.*

I had an extra pep in my step as I walked to the office from the train station. "Ma'am?" I heard from behind me on the sidewalk. I turned around. I found myself locking eyes with a handsome, younger African American man who was wearing a backpack, a hoodie and jeans. I guessed he was on his way to school.

"Yes?"

"I just wanted to tell you. You're beautiful." My cheeks flushed. I hadn't received a compliment like that in years. He was charming, but he seemed about ten years too young for me.

"Aw, well, thank you," I said a little awkwardly. "Um, I have to get to work." I quickly turned and kept walking. *You're really slick, Vanessa. Good one.* I rolled my eyes at my own awkwardness. The universe was already bringing it on.

I kept my head focused on work, which passed quickly with so much data to sort through. I made a pretty great technical analyst, I thought. But I was starting to miss the direct client interaction I used to have. 5 pm arrived before I knew it, and as I was packing up, I started saying a mantra in my head that I'd just read about in the book. *I am connected to everyone and everything.* It took a little longer than usual getting down the elevator, and I checked my watch. 5:07. I needed to catch the 5:15 train home to be back to Zach around 6. Once out of the elevator and onto the street, I started picking up the pace to a slight jog. *I am connected to everyone and everything,* I repeated to myself. It was 5:10, and I still had to go all the way down the length of the train tracks from the north end and make a U-turn onto one of the other platforms that wasn't accessible from the stairs I'd come down. I started to make it into a full run at this point, while still repeating the mantra in my head. *I am connected to everyone and everything.*

"Don't be late, gorgeous!" A man's voice in the distance interrupted my thoughts. I thought he might be talking to me, but I couldn't slow down. I zipped right by him and could only tell that he was well dressed in a suit. I kept running and made it to my platform at 5:14, with just a minute to spare.

"Phew!" I said to the train conductor as I got on board, panting to catch my breath. "Glad you didn't leave without me!"

"You barely made it," he chuckled at me.

I threw my bags down in an empty row and sat in the window seat, looking at the platform I'd just sprinted through. I saw a few people standing there waiting for their train, including the man in a business suit peering towards the train. For a moment we made eye contact. He smiled and gave a small wave.

Amazing. What magic am I unleashing with this book?

I thought about what Cathy and I talked about this morning. She seemed to think I had my swagger back, and after today, I had to agree. I grabbed my laptop and connected it to the internet from my phone. Without hesitation, I went to Match.com and signed up for a subscription. *Are you out there, Mr. Wonderful? I'm looking for you!*

I finally arrived home just after 6. I put down my bag and took off my jacket, ready to hold Zach as soon as possible. "Here's your baby!" Cathy said, smiling, handing him to me.

"Girl, I have no idea what was in the air today, but from the feel of it, the magic is happening now, and I am ready to go for it. It's insane, in an awesome way! I signed up for Match on the way home from work!"

She giggled. "Okay, Vanessa, you definitely are ready. Did you write a profile?"

"No, not yet, I need some time to think. I want it to be really good. It's more important than a resume, isn't it? It's an introduction to the love of my life! Can you proofread it for me when I'm done? And... I need a photo!"

"Yeah I was thinking about this today. You know, you have Zach's six-month photos set up for next week, why don't you just ask the photographer to do a quick headshot of you while she's at it? That's all you really need, right?

"You're a genius. Right. Let's plan for it. You're coming with me to the shoot, right?"

"I wouldn't miss it for the world." She was the most amazing, supportive friend I could have asked for.

I spent the next few weeks writing my Match.com profile in my spare time on the train. It now had been a full year since life had pulled out the rug from underneath me. My support group planned a meet up for Valentine's Day dinner at a Greek restaurant. It was a smaller group of about six women. We caught up on recent battle stories with our exes, had some laughs, and enjoyed the food and wine together.

"Vanessa, you are totally glowing," my friend Abby told me. "If I had to guess, I'd say that you'd met someone!"

"Seriously, what have you been doing? You seem so happy!" Jane interjected.

"Well, I haven't met anyone... at least not yet. But I'm about to, and I can feel it. I've been focusing on forgiveness, so I can really move on and find the right guy with no strings attached...." I told my girlfriends about the breakthrough I'd made when I wrote my gratitude list of what I was thankful for in my marriage, and how focusing on the good things had set me free. I mentioned to them that I'd also recently been utilizing a Hawaiian practice of forgiveness called *Ho'oponopono* and that this had surprisingly shifted me into a place of peace more quickly than I'd imagined. The entire practice was based around four simple statements. "I'm sorry. Please forgive me. Thank you. I love you." The idea was to think about the person that you had trouble forgiving and repeat these lines over and over again as you focused on them.

The girls at the table sat there in disbelief. "So, let me get this straight. Your key to happiness is asking *him* for forgiveness?" Abby dropped her fork on her plate. "I don't think I could do that. I mean, after all he did to you, he should be the one asking for forgiveness, right?"

"Yes, I know it sounds crazy, but I decided to flip the script. Wouldn't it be interesting to be the one asking for forgiveness? I'm not even saying it to his face; I'm just meditating about it. And I have to tell you, I'm feeling 100% better after doing it, and that's all that really matters." This was the magic of the healing process – owning my part in the demise of my marriage and realizing that I was not everything that *he* had needed in a partner. I truly was sorry for my part in this and any pain I had caused and wished him the best. In some sense, Dylan was one of my greatest teachers. The feeling of abandonment in my most fragile state as a young mother when he walked away resulted in the greatest learning strides of my life, and without them, I would never know how strong I was. My heart was broken wide open and there was nothing else to do but embrace the broken pieces that built this mosaic of my life.

"Here's the funny thing," I continued. "I had to do this forgiveness thing with myself too. I processed a lot of shame over the past few months, and I've finally let myself off the hook. I mean, being a single mom and Catholic, that left me in a conundrum for a long time. And you know what? I forgave myself. I also forgave myself for the largeness of my ego since I had assumed for years that I had this life thing figured out. When everything fell apart, I had to find humility and accept that I was beginner level student of life. I re-learned how to wake up in the morning and get out of bed, how to get through each day, and applauded myself for taking one step at a time. I'm really proud of how far I've come."

My friends were all listening intently, waiting for more. "Now that I'm through all that, I'm making it loud and clear to the universe that I'm ready to find my real partner in life. And you know what? He's on the way to me right now, I can feel it. I can't describe it any other way than there's a *knowing* I have about all this. I cannot wait to meet him!"

"Wow, cheers to that, girlfriend!" my friend Rose said, raising her glass to me. I met it with mine.

"Cheers to us! To falling in love with ourselves!" I responded back. We all raised our glasses to celebrate.

The morning following Valentine's dinner, I finished my Match.com profile, a rush of excitement coming over me as I uploaded photos and published the following profile:

I won the lottery once but decided to rip up the ticket for fun. Okay, not really. But I sold my 2005 World Series tickets to attend a friend's wedding in Santa Fe, and I think I now understand the feeling. Oh, those friends still owe me, but what can I say? These are the things you do for the people you love. I believe that in life, you have to take chances to experience the extraordinary. Watching shooting stars at the top of a mountain, tasting exquisite cuisine in Calistoga, doing a photoshoot at Rancho Nambe that helped me realize my camera truly is an extension of my Spirit... It's not just about leaving town to take the road less traveled, though. I once dropped out of college to start a career in an all-girl band (think: Spice Girls, the Chicago version). And while I'm not a member of the Pussycat Dolls today, the good news is, I had some killer backup dancer moves to "Sexyback" to entertain my friends at Lincoln Karaoke last weekend. (Well, at least I have my career in product data management to keep me gainfully employed.) It's been an interesting ride, but life truly began when I had my son. When I look at him, I know that I'm exactly where I'm meant to be and that God and the universe are amazingly good. I'm looking forward to the adventure of new love because while there are other types of relationships to be had, I know true love is what I'm meant to find.

Okay, Mr. Wonderful, I know you're out there. Here's what you feel like to me: You are confident with your place in the world. You set high goals for yourself and work hard to achieve them. You look people in the eye when you speak to them. You share my passion for self-growth because you also believe it's important to keep learning and improving. You'd trust me to help you test out the website for your new business, because you know I'd do anything I could to help you achieve your dreams. You'd be up for a run through the forest preserve on a beautiful fall day. You wouldn't mind me photographing you as I test out camera equipment. You'd humor me if I asked you to review a couple of PowerPoint slides for my next client presentation. You'd consider taking dance lessons or cooking lessons with me. You'd teach me something new. You make children laugh. You have faith.

There was one more section to fill out, called a *tagline*. I filled it in with a line from my favorite Spice Girls song, "So, tell me what you want, what you really, really want…"

I'd completely accepted the fact that I might end up going on 50 bad dates but knew the bright side was that I'd have hilarious stories to tell my friends later. Keeping zero expectations, I would allow the universe to surprise me. Maybe I'd make some friends; maybe I would actually fall in love. Who knows?

Hours after activating my account, Cathy was over to begin the day, and I was preparing to leave for work. "I'm officially available on Match.com!" I exclaimed as she walked into my office.

"What? No way! Let me see!" She almost shoved me over so she could take a look at the computer screen. I started laughing.

"Okay, okay, let me give you the tour." I was still logged in, so I showed her around on the site. I had already received three new messages.

"How are you gonna work this?" she asked with her arms leaning into the desk and turning her head to me intently.

"Well, I'm still working that out. I am not going to jump to meet anyone in person until I'm sure there's potential. I don't know how I'll be sure, but we'll figure it out, right?"

"Okay, don't meet anyone at night," she cautioned. "Just let them come meet you at lunchtime downtown. That just seems safer."

"You're totally right. And I don't have to figure out a babysitter for that! I think we have a plan!"

Within a week, I had received a mailbox full of introduction emails and had started talking to a few people on the phone. The universe was definitely delivering an abundance of men. The next step was finding "The One."

Chapter 12: March Madness

In the large conference room at work one morning, my co-worker Ryan and I were meeting to review some of the analysis I'd been working on for his project. Ryan had become a close pal in recent months, and he knew that I was about to start my new dating adventure. With his thick black-rimmed glasses and sharp tongue, he reminded me of a smarter version of Dwight from the show *The Office.*

I had my laptop projecting onto the wall as we wrapped up our conversation. "Good for now?" I asked.

"Yes, ma'am. Nice work, thank you."

"Sounds good. Let me know when you hear back from Jenn on those two deviations, and we'll make sure to document them exactly the same way."

"Cool. Hey, how's your Match.com adventure going? Did you pick any winners yet?"

"Dude, I am having the time of my life! I am chatting with a few different guys, but I haven't met anyone in person yet."

"Why not?"

"Well, it's been less than a week. To be honest, I haven't figured out how to handle the meeting in person part yet."

"Interesting," he said, raising an eyebrow at me. "I have an idea." He picked up a dry-erase marker and stood next to the large whiteboard. "How many guys so far? What are their names?"

"It's easier if I give you their nicknames." I pulled up my Match.com account so he could see, scrolling through some of my messages. "So far, there are... six of them. There's Cupcake Guy, Scrabble Guy, Forrester Guy, Belize guy, Giant Guy, and just this weekend, I started messaging with Martial Arts Guy."

Ryan drew four lines on one side of the board, and another four on the other side. He started writing names on the lines and started drawing brackets around pairs of names.

"You're definitely going to keep meeting more guys, so I'm saving two spots in the bracket." At the top of the board, he wrote March Madness. He was clearly making a pun on the National Collegiate Athletic Association (NCAA) college tournaments. "I think we can get a little inter-office wagering going on here," he giggled. "Who will make it to the final four?" he said, putting his fingers to his cheeks and rolling his eyes, seeming to mock the voice of a teenage girl. I broke out into full out laughter.

"I think it's supposed to be the Sweet Sixteen in there, but I'll settle for eight for now!"

"At the rate you're going, we might have to make it sixteen, but yeah, let's start here." He chuckled again. "I'm telling our team we can start accepting bets now."

Just then, a new message came in from match. It was a Martial Arts Guy.

I looked up at Ryan. "Holy crap. It's Martial Arts Guy. He's coming downtown today, and he's wondering if we could meet up for coffee."

"Heh! Perfect timing! Go meet him!"

"Ryan, I am *not* dressed for a first date." I grabbed his arm urgently. "Ugh! And I'm having a bad hair day! Look at this!" I pointed to the top of my head where I was sure some baby hairs were sticking straight up.

"Who cares? Just go have fun. Gotta have the first date sooner or later, no time like the present!"

Martial Arts Guy was actually named Jeremy, and we had been messaging over the weekend. I was surprised at how quickly he was growing on me, easily becoming the one I was most interested in. Most of the guys I was talking to were very outwardly flirtatious, but in messaging with Jeremy, it felt like he was just a genuinely sweet guy. There were no games going on. He had two sons from a previous marriage. He was a civil engineer and ran his own small business. He loved photography and Brazilian Jiu-Jitsu and was quite involved in his local mixed martial arts gym. He lived in a far suburb called Algonquin, which I'd never heard of before. I'd wondered all weekend if he was ever going to ask for my phone number. So far, he hadn't.

I started typing a response to Jeremy. "Hey there! Glad to hear you'll be in my neck of the woods. Give me a ring if you're still around, and we could try to meet up." I typed in my number.

"Hey, we're walking down to the Citibank building for lunch. Are you coming?" Ryan asked, looking down at his laptop. He was typing quickly, chatting with a few of our colleagues online.

Closing my laptop, I responded. "Yeah, I'm coming, wait for me..." I ran out of the conference room to grab my coat and purse at my desk and met my colleagues at the elevator.

When we returned from lunch, I realized I hadn't actually sent the message to Jeremy yet. I lingered a few seconds, wondering if it was too forward of me to hand out my phone number without him asking. I re-read my message.

"No time like the present..." I thought, hitting *send.*

After half an hour, I received a text message on my phone from a number I didn't recognize.

> **Jeremy:** Hi, it's Jeremy. There must be a delay in the Match email delivery, but I left the city already. How does your Friday look?

Dang. After building up my courage, I had missed him. Part of me was relieved, though; I still had a chance to meet him on a good hair day.

> **Me:** Friday works at lunchtime, how about you? I would be up for coffee normally but already have that scheduled with my CEO in the afternoon, and there's only so much coffee a girl can drink in a day!

When I'd come back from maternity leave, my company had announced a merger with another company, and as part of that, a few of us were invited to one-on-one meetings with the new CEO.

Jeremy agreed to lunch, and though I half expected him to call me that evening, my phone did not ring. *Okay, guess I can wait till Friday,* I told myself.

At home later that evening, I fed Zach rice cereal in his high-chair and talked to my parents over dinner. My baby was already eight months old and eating like a champion, and I had become a pro at getting most of the food in his mouth without it falling onto his shirt or bib. I kissed his nose, and he giggled.

"So…" I said, grinning, turning to my mom. "I may be going on a date soon."

My mom stopped eating and looked at me, a bit shocked. "What? You're still *married*." Her face was completely serious, and she looked at me with her eyebrows furrowed in concern.

"Mom, *come on*. I'm not really married. We're getting divorced. It's only on paper that we are still married, and he has clearly moved on. I'm ready to move on too." Zach was slapping his hand on the table, asking for more food. I scooped another spoonful into his mouth.

"But the baby is so young, and your marriage is still recognized by the Catholic Church. I think it's considered a sin to do such things."

I was flustered. My mom was a stickler for rules, especially when it came to Catholicism. I knew this was an argument that I wasn't bound to win. "Well, I'm caught in man-made rules of the church then. I don't think there's a handbook for what I've been through,

Mom. I'm pretty proud of how far I've come. And I don't think God would judge me for moving on with my life."

She sighed softly. "I know, baby. I am proud of you too. You are a good mom. You love your son. I just don't know what the rules are about this. I don't want you to be seen poorly in the eyes of the church. It's already enough that you're getting divorced. You should get an annulment first, and maybe then it will be okay to start dating again when the time is right, and the baby is older."

"Mom, who knows how long annulment will take? It could be years! If I want to move on and have more kids in the future, my clock is ticking. I deserve to have the family I want, and I'm ready to start figuring that out now. I can't possibly believe there's something sinful about that." I took a deep breath, realizing I was getting too upset. "Look, Mom, I know this is an issue for you. I'll go talk to Father Dennis and see if he can give me any guidance here."

I looked at my dad, who was only halfway listening to us and had his eyes on the television. "Dad, what do you think?"

"About what?" he asked, probably wishing he wasn't part of this conversation.

"About me dating."

"Who are you going to meet?"

"There's a guy I'm talking to named Jeremy."

"How do you know him?"

"From an online dating site."

"You met a man on the internet?" His eyes were wide with surprise. Straight-faced, he looked at me and then erupted in laughter, a big hearty belly laugh.

I started laughing too, relieved he at least didn't seem to be disappointed in me. "I know you think that's funny, dad, but I don't have time to hang out at random places to try to find the right man." I poked him in the ribs with my elbow.

He put his arm around me and squeezed me. "If you're ready, I don't think it's a problem. But talk to Father Dennis. Your mom will feel better." He winked at me. He was listening after all.

I knew deep in my bones that I was ready. I was not going to change my mind about meeting Jeremy or any other man for that matter. And I knew it wasn't wrong of me to want this for myself. But I hated the thought of my mother not approving, and I wanted her to be with me on this.

On Friday morning, I got up a little earlier than usual and spent some extra time to get ready before work. *This is going to be a great day.* I'd spoken to Fr. Dennis the night before, and he'd given me the green light. "As long as you feel emotionally ready, it's perfectly healthy and natural for you to want to meet someone new," he'd advised me. "There's nothing wrong with meeting men and dating." I'd skipped downstairs that evening and informed my mother, feeling like a kid whose teacher had just given her an A+. His approval had appeased my mother's concerns, and I felt better not having to deal with the internal conflict so I could date in peace. Staring at myself in the mirror that morning, I made sure my eyebrows were freshly plucked, and my makeup was perfect, even going as far as wearing some mascara, which I didn't normally do. I picked a black V-neck satin top that I cinched around the waist with a thick black belt. I wore a pair of my favorite dark wash tapered jeans and some high heel suede boots. With my white and black hooded jacket, I thought the whole outfit looked pretty cute. I said a little prayer as I walked out the door, holding my rosary in my hand. I envisioned myself laughing easily with this new person over lunch, exuding confidence, and genuinely enjoying myself.

Once I arrived at work that morning there were a flurry of last-minute emergencies, and I found myself rushing from one meeting to the next. While I was sitting in Ali's office around 11 AM, I received a text from Jeremy.

> **Jeremy:** Hi Vanessa! I'm in the city. Where should I meet you at noon?

Butterflies started swirling around in my stomach again as I wrote to suggest we meet at Thai Urban Kitchen. *A first date!* I hadn't been on a first date in over a decade! I wrapped up my meeting as soon as I could and started mentally preparing myself to meet Jeremy. At 11:45, I made a stop in the women's lounge area in the restroom at work, carefully checking myself in the mirror. *Did I look okay? Was there anything in my teeth? Oh my god, I have ten minutes before I meet this guy!* I checked myself in the mirror. Smoothing my hair over, I smiled. *Only one chance to make a first impression*, I thought. I headed out toward the elevator, then made a U-turn, and marched right back into the ladies' room. Taking a deep breath, I stared myself down in the mirror. "You've got this." I coached myself. "Just have fun. Be funny! You're funny, aren't you? Be *interesting*. Be *interested*. And whatever you do, *don't talk about the ex*." I pointed at myself in the mirror as I said this. And with that, I walked out of the office, shoulders pulled back, and head held high, ready to meet him finally. On the way to the elevator this time, I bumped into Ryan. "Like my first date outfit?" I said as I twirled around once and pressed the elevator button.

"Go get 'em, tiger!" he quipped. "Stick to the plan, and we'll send out the search party if you're not back in a reasonable time frame." He said with one eyebrow raised.

"Yessir!"

I approached the Citibank building at the corner of Madison and Canal, walking towards my favorite restaurant in the area. Peering through the windows, I saw the place was bustling with the usual lunch crowd. I caught a glimpse of an Asian man sitting by himself looking at his phone. My heart was pounding. That *might* be him.

"Keep going," I told myself. "This is it - the next step in your life. Just have fun!" Walking into the building, I walked past the Hudson Bookstore, and turned right towards the restaurant, pausing at the front door. The man I'd seen through the window stood up and waved at me. It was Jeremy!

"Here goes nothing," I muttered to myself as I smiled and waved back. He was wearing a black sweater and dark pants. He looked casual but sophisticated, and oddly enough, we looked like we were dressed to match. I walked towards him.

"Hi there!" I said confidently, with a smile beaming from my face. I sat down at the table across from him. "I hope you weren't waiting too long."

"Not at all. Hi, Vanessa," he said with a big smile and a bit of a nervous laugh. *Wow.* He was handsome. Even cuter than in the photos I'd seen. Up close, I could see he was wearing a Hugo Boss sweater. *Good sense of style,* I thought. He had a beautiful smile and perfect white teeth. He had moved to the bench across from me with his back against the window, and I now sat in the chair he had been sitting when I saw him from outside. I nervously tried to figure out where to put my purse. I hadn't thought about that beforehand. As I was about to opt to put it on the floor, Jeremy noticed my predicament. "Do you want to switch seats?" he offered.

Biting my lip, I responded. "Um, yes, I would. Thanks." I stood up to put my purse down on the bench where he was sitting and took my jacket off, laying it on top of the purse. He was already thoughtful. As he stood up, I could see he was about six inches taller than me, a pretty comfortable height difference. He was slim, and he looked very fit. Sitting down again, we locked eyes for a moment. I had to catch my breath.

"So… did you stay up late again to watch *Dexter*?" I asked. We'd been chatting about the TV show over the weekend, and I had almost ruined one of the seasons for him accidentally. He grinned at me.

"Not last night. I had to try to look decent for our date today." He looked down at his outfit and then looked up at me again and smiled. "But it's been a nice escape to watch the show when the kids are sleeping."

"I bet. I miss TV. I haven't had much time to watch since having the baby."

"Are you ready to order?" A waitress had come by to check in on us. I looked at Jeremy, "I'm ready, are you?"

"Sure, you go ahead."

"The sushi combo number one, please."

"I'll have the panang curry."

The waitress responded, "Okay, I'll get your order in." she quickly turned around and walked away.

Jeremy started chuckling. "You invited me to a Thai place to order sushi."

I laughed. "Well, yes, I guess I did. I'm not eating meat today since it's a Friday, and it's Lent," I explained. "And honestly, I could eat sushi every day."

"Oh, that's right. Are you religious?"

"Fairly religious, I guess. I go to church regularly, and I try to stick to the basics. I'd say I'm spiritual. How about you?"

"I'm Catholic too, but I have to admit I haven't been practicing much for the past year or so. I just started going back to mass recently ...So tell me, what do you do at your company? Are you an analyst?"

"Well, kind of. I manage projects for our consulting engagements, and I oversee implementations of our own technology as well as third-party software. More recently, since I got back from maternity leave, I've been doing some work as an IT analyst for our technology team." I added, "Where I used to be in front of clients 100% of the time, now I get to sit in a conference room at work cranking out spreadsheets all day. It's good for the time being, but eventually, I'll get back to my normal day job as a people person. For now, though, I'm rocking out V-lookups like nobody's business."

He laughed out loud. "Watch out, next you'll be doing pivot tables!"

"Oh, don't go there. Those are way too technical for me!" I laughed.

I looked at him intently. "I'm curious, what is a day like for you? I know you said you're a civil engineer, but I have to be honest, I have no idea what that's like."

"Right," he said and laughed again. "Well I run a couple of different businesses. I'm a civil engineer, and I work in water and wastewater specifically. I design water treatment plants, and I also run an operations business. On a normal day, I'm having my guys get water samples, and I'm out in the field a lot with them. I go out to see clients regularly too, so I'm in the car for what seems like most of the day."

We talked about work for a while. I was intrigued by learning about what he did, as it was a completely different world than mine. As it turned out, he not only designed water treatment plants but was also involved in the construction phase of those projects. He smiled a lot as I asked him questions. I was enjoying his company. He was really an interesting guy - very smart and very confident. I asked him more about martial arts too. One of his best friends was a UFC fighter, and so he knew a lot of people in the MMA world.

"So, I'm curious," I said between bites of my salmon roll. "I'm new to this Match thing and am just figuring out how this all works. How long have you been using this site?"

"On and off for the past year or so," he mentioned, not missing a beat. "Just hadn't found anyone that seemed to fit right. I've met three or four people, including you."

"Cool. Well, this is my first date, and I wasn't sure what to expect! I've met a lot of people online, but you're the first one I'm meeting in person."

Eventually, I told him that my co-workers were in on my Match.com adventure and that we weren't really here alone, per se. I had spotted one of my co-workers walking by, and he'd peered in the window and seen me.

"Just in case you're a serial killer, there are several people in the immediate vicinity that know what you look like and where we're sitting. If I don't return to my office in an acceptable timeframe, they'll be looking for me here."

He laughed heartily. "Well, you certainly have a plan."

"Always." I quipped. "So, how do your kids like jiu-jitsu? My little guy is only eight months old, so he's too young for any activities like that." I wondered if it would bother him that I had a baby and watched his face closely, convinced this was one of those things that scared a guy away. He didn't flinch.

"Ah, my guys just have fun learning. It's good to keep them active in martial arts to learn discipline. But they do just end up playing around a lot sometimes. They'll get it more when they get older. I just like to keep them active and moving. Tell me about *your* little guy."

Instinctively, I grabbed my phone and found his six-month photos that we'd recently taken, bragging about how chubby his cheeks were and how great he was doing at Gymboree classes. Jeremy reached over to take my phone and have a closer look. For a moment, our fingers touched, and I was pretty sure my cheeks flushed. He held my phone closer and was looking at a black and white photo of me holding Zachary, who had a white button-down shirt and tie on. He flashed his smile at me again.

"He's a cutie!"

"No doubt!" I smiled, my enthusiasm for my son momentarily relieving me of my nervousness.

Jeremy reached down and grabbed his phone out of his jacket pocket. He pulled up a photo and gave me his phone. "These are my guys," he beamed. The older one's name is Johan, and the younger one is Zakri." The name stopped me in my tracks. I looked up at him.

"My son's name is Zachary!"

He smiled. "Yes, they're similar names, but not exactly the same. It's spelled Z-A-K-R-I and is two syllables, pronounced 'Zah-kree.' It's a Malaysian name."

"Well, they are both *adorable*," I remarked, zooming in on their faces. It was a photo of his two sons at the beach, wearing matching blue swim trunks and Quicksilver rash guards. Johan was missing his two front teeth, and Zakri had cheeks that might give my Zach a run for his money. "Look at the size of those cheeks on Zakri! That's impressive!"

Jeremy showed me a few more photos of him and his boys, talking about one of their recent trips to San Diego. He was clearly a very hands-on dad, and it was obvious the kids were his main priority.

"Excuse me, can I have a few extra napkins?" he said to the waitress as she walked by. "This curry is spicy," he said to me after she walked away. "It's making my head sweat." I hadn't noticed before, but beads of sweat were forming at the top of his forehead, and I offered him my napkin.

"Woah, are you okay? You're sweating buckets!" I laughed.

"Yeah, I love spicy food," he said, laughing, "But it comes at a cost. It tastes good, though!"

Lunch went by quickly, and before I knew it, I had to get back to work. Jeremy took the bill as soon as it came and paid for it. As he stood up, he put on a sporty black Hugo Boss jacket and a Kangol wool baseball hat. I loved his style. I zipped up my coat as we walked out of the restaurant, and he let me walk ahead of him following me out the door. As we pushed through the revolving doors and the winter cold swept across my face, I quickly snapped back into work mode, remembering I was meeting with my new CEO soon. For a split second, I felt Jeremy lightly put his hand on my lower back as we headed toward the sidewalk. I walked next to him, accidentally stepping a little too close and brushed my shoulder against his arm. He had put his hands in his pockets, and I did the same.

"Are you parked close?" I asked.

"Yeah, just down the street here," he said, pointing down Canal Street. I remembered Ryan warning me not to let anyone know which building I worked in, just in case they ended up being creepy. I wasn't sure how to end the date, and we were approaching the closest intersection to my building. A bit awkwardly, I spit out, "I've gotta run to that meeting. Talk to you later, bye!" and I waved as I headed down the block, not looking back. Moments later, in the safety of my familiar elevator going back up to the 20th floor, I took deep breaths and looked at my reflection in the elevator wall. *I did it!* I smiled at myself, wanting to give myself a high five. I wished I had been a little smoother with my exit but tried to salvage it with a follow-up text.

Me: Thank you for lunch! I had a great time!

He messaged me right back.

Jeremy: Same here! I would love to see you again. Have a good meeting!

I smiled to myself as I walked back to my desk. Scott, the co-worker who sat directly across from my cube, noticed my smile as I walked over, and he looked amused. "Ooooh - It's just lunch!" he quipped from over the wall, referring to a dating site with a smirk on his face. "I can see Martial Arts guy did well! You're glowing!" My March Madness brackets had obviously made the rounds at the office. Just then, Ryan walked by and saw the look on my face. My co-workers and I huddled up and debriefed on date number one. I told them Jeremy would definitely be advancing to the next round.

"Easy there, sister," Ryan interjected. "You have to date two different guys before you advance someone to the next round." He chuckled. "Okay, I'm kidding. It's up to you. But you really are glowing."

"All right, smarty-pants," I retorted. "I already have Cupcake Guy zeroing in on a date for next week, so let's just see how that goes. The Giant Guy is not too far behind either…"

"Excellent."

"Okay, kids, I'm off to my coffee meeting with the boss. And no, he's not on the brackets," I laughed. Though I seemed gung-ho on dating other guys, I was pretty smitten with this incredible man I'd just met. I found myself replaying the date in my head for the rest of the afternoon, which helped the rest of the day cruise by while I started on the next round of spreadsheet analysis. On the train home that night, I received another text from Jeremy:

> **Jeremy:** You should tell your co-workers I'm really weird.

I laughed out loud, typing back quickly.

> **Me:** You are. That's what I told everyone.

He responded right away:

> **Jeremy:** Ha-ha, perfect.

> **Me:** What are you up to?

> **Jeremy:** At the gym waiting for the boys to stop playing in the cage. They finished training and are throwing all of Zakri's toys around. Help me. What about you?

> **Me:** On the train, almost home. Miss my boy!

> **Jeremy:** Awww, he's so pudgy. He's going to be a tank!

> **Me:** No, kidding! Sometimes I wonder if he's eating too much.
>
> **Jeremy:** Eh - it's good to be the big kid. Do you speak Tagalog?

I'd mentioned to him I was Filipino while we were talking earlier today.

> **Me:** Only swear words.
>
> **Jeremy:** Cute. Good because I don't have time to learn a foreign language.
>
> **Me:** I keep forgetting to ask you what nationality are you?

My entire life, my parents had never had an expectation for me to marry an Asian guy, which I guess made me an exception to the rule. While I'd dated Latinos and Caucasian men in the past, oddly enough, it was usually Asian men I was most attracted to.

> **Jeremy:** Taiwanese. I can't speak it though, just understand. You know, I think you shortchanged yourself on match saying you are 4'11". I'm pretty sure I'm 5'6" and I thought you were going to be really short.
>
> **Me:** I'm 4'11.5" and I wear high heels, but let's not get too technical.
>
> **Jeremy:** I would have rounded up, not down. Who's the weird one now?

I liked that he was giving me a hard time, and figured I'd give it back.

Me: So, if I round up, will I be more marketable on match, you think?!

Jeremy: No comment.

Me: Screw it, I'm putting 6'5"

Jeremy: Yes - and big and beautiful. Please make that change. Put unemployed too while you're at it. You are insanely pretty, but don't write that.

I blushed. I guess we were equally smitten with each other. We made a date for lunch the following week before signing off for the evening.

Jeremy: Good night, Bebot Girl.

He was referring to my Match.com profile, where I used the term Bebot, a popular song by the Black-Eyed Peas. Bebot (pronounced Beh-boht) means "hot chick" or "babe" in Tagalog. I liked that he threw that in there. After putting the baby to bed, I fell asleep with a smile on my face.

On Saturday night, I dropped off Zach with Dylan for his weekend visit. Though it was never something I looked forward to, leaving my baby for the evening was getting easier. I wasn't living the life I'd imagined a few years ago, but I was living in the flow now and actually enjoying it. This weekend, I had plans to meet up with my girlfriends for dinner at one of my favorite restaurants in the city, Fiesta Mexicana. This was becoming a regular spot for us, and we had plans to go dancing at a bar across the street afterward. Over some delicious chimichangas and some strawberry margaritas, I talked about how my first date had gone and got a full table of high fives congratulating me on moving on. With full bellies and full hearts, my girlfriends and I danced the night away.

The next morning, my family decided to meet for lunch in the Glen. My parents were about to leave on another two-week trip, this time to Ecuador, which meant Zach and I would have the house to ourselves again.

"So, Vaness, tell me about this date you had?" my brother asked as he slurped up some noodles. We sat across from each other at the restaurant, using the little time we had together to our advantage. I held Zach in my lap and was feeding him little bites of my chicken soup.

"Well, I met this guy on Match. His name is Jeremy, and he's a civil engineer. He owns his own business. He's divorced with two little boys. He's also really into jiu-jitsu." I made sure to mention the jiu-jitsu part since my brother's sons also trained jiu-jitsu. Zach was slapping the table, reminding me to feed him some noodles too.

"Oh yeah? Where does he train? I wonder if I know his gym." David had grown up doing Muay Thai kickboxing and had a deep respect for martial arts.

"It's all the way out in Crystal Lake. I'm gonna guess you wouldn't know his gym. But yeah, he and his boys train jiu-jitsu every week. He seems to be a very involved dad and puts those kids first."

"I see, that's good. Is he Catholic?"

"Yes. He is." I smiled at him. I knew my brother was rooting for me to find a fellow Catholic. I, on the other hand, had cast my net pretty wide and wasn't attached to my partner being of any particular religion.

"Sounds like a good guy to me," he said, reaching over to pick up his youngest daughter, Olivia, who was stirring in her stroller, waking up from a nap. He was convinced, and I was relieved. Maybe this would rub off on my mom, who still seemed a little hesitant about me dating.

Later that afternoon, I logged back onto Match.com. I felt like I wasn't doing my homework if I didn't do my daily half-hour on the website catching up with the other guys I'd been messaging. Cupcake Guy, whose real name was Mark, was a cop with the Chicago Police Department. He suggested lunch the following week, but something in me told me to hold off. As Scrabble Guy and Forrester Guy also reached out that evening to try to make plans, I found myself stalling for time. The truth was, I just wanted to see Jeremy again.

The following Tuesday night, as I was getting Zach situated in my car after picking him up from Dylan, my phone rang. It was Jeremy.

"Hey, how was your day?" he asked. I was still getting used to the sound of his voice. It was loud and seemed to cut right through a room, and I had to adjust the volume down a little so that it wouldn't interrupt my baby.

"Hi Jeremy! It's good to hear your voice. I'm doing well! Just picked up my son, and we're on the drive home. How are you?"

"I'm good, thanks, just heading home myself. The boys had jiu-jitsu tonight. Where are you picking up your little guy?"

"Oh, at church, not too far from home. He sees his father on Tuesday nights, and this has been our handoff location."

"Oh interesting. Why did you guys pick the church as your drop off place?"

Without thinking it through, I started giving Jeremy the cliff notes version of what had happened leading up to my breakup with Dylan. I did not plan for this to be something we talked about until later, but as I started explaining, Jeremy asked more questions, and before I knew it, he had the full unedited story. We ended up talking for about half an hour, and I drove around the neighborhood in circles, hoping that Zach would be okay as I continued to talk on the extra-long drive home. As I paused to collect my thoughts, my heart was pounding. I wondered if I'd shared too much, but it was too late to take it back. On the other end of the line, I heard Jeremy start laughing. *What in the world could be so funny about this?*

"Why are you laughing?" I asked, honestly. *Did he think I was joking?*

"Sorry, I just, I guess I'm just surprised at how dramatic your story is. I'm sorry for what you've been through. It seems like you've had to handle quite a bit."

I felt completely exposed, foolish for sharing this much. "I know it's a lot of drama. I've been through a lot. Hey listen, I'm just getting home, and I need to take care of my son. I'll talk to you later, okay?" Hot tears were streaming down my face. I was ashamed I'd shared so much and wished I could take the words back. I was sure he'd be backing away from me as soon as he could. I probably seemed like a mess. A girl with baggage. After the strides I'd taken up to this point in my life, I knew that wasn't who I was.

I focused the rest of my evening intensely on Zach and tried to forget about everything that had just happened. Rocking him to sleep, I whispered in his ear, "Go to sleep, my sweet boy. Mama will always be here for you, I promise. You are going to have a better life than I ever knew possible, just wait and see. It's just you and me kiddo…" I kissed both of his eyelids as he finally went down for the night.

As I was drifting off to sleep at around 11 pm, I heard my phone buzz. A message popped up from Jeremy:

> **Jeremy:** Hey, thanks for sharing your story with me. It's not lost upon me what you may be going through. I just love talking with you :)

A wave of relief rushed over me. I hadn't scared him away.

> **Me:** Sorry, it just spilled out. It's a pretty ugly story, I know. Despite that, I don't subscribe to the victim mentality these days. I don't need someone to save me or anything, and I hope it didn't come across that way. And, thanks for understanding.

> **Jeremy:** Not at all. I'm sure you have your moments, especially with all the things he said. I tend to laugh at stuff if you didn't notice, but it's more for levity, and I can certainly feel for your situation.

As I was reading his last message, my phone rang. It was him. "Hi again," I answered, almost whispering.

"Hey, sorry to call so late. I just wanted to hear your voice." He sounded quieter this time. "I guess we've both been through a lot, and I can certainly relate to the pains of divorce." Jeremy started sharing his story this time. He'd been married to his ex-wife for almost a decade. They had also been college sweethearts. Their relationship had been tumultuous from the beginning, often getting into explosive arguments, which only got worse when their first baby arrived.

"Looking back at it now, I can see that our personalities never clicked in the first place. It's hard to see that when you're so deep into it. I guess we were both trying so hard to force it to work. I can barely remember that decade of my life; it was like I lost myself. After a while, we ended up living separated but in the same house for a year, then as we went through the divorce, she moved out, and it took another year to get through the proceedings."

"Wow. Thanks for sharing with me," I told him, "That really dragged out for a long time. I'm so sorry for what you've been through, but it sounds like you have your priorities straight. You're a great dad. And I completely agree, it's hard to see it when you're in it. It took me the better part of a year to learn to forgive myself for that."

"Yep. Well, I could talk to you all night, but I think we better get some sleep. I may be opening up a new martial arts gym downtown, and we're meeting about it tomorrow night."

"Woah, that sounds amazing. But yes, I'm beat. Let's talk more tomorrow; I'd love to hear more about this new gym!"

When we hung up that evening, I was even more intrigued by this man than I was the day before. I wondered if I'd be able to see him at all if he was downtown, if only for a couple of minutes. I didn't want to wait until Friday.

Since I seemed to be in the business of blurting things out lately, I sent a text to Jeremy the next afternoon:

> **Me:** Is it bad that I want to see you? Bad. Ugh.
>
> **Jeremy:** Well, it's mutual. You better not cancel on Friday!

He mentioned that he was heading downtown with his friend and couldn't stop to see me since they had an appointment and then dinner scheduled. Slightly embarrassed, I walked down to the train station to catch the next train back to Morton Grove. I wondered if the people on the train could sense that I'd just made two dating faux pas in a row. Sinking into my seat on the train, I felt my phone buzz again.

> **Jeremy:** Have a nice evening! I'll catch up with you later tonight if that's ok Vanessa Schmanessa :)

Now having an opening to recover, I retorted back.

> **Me:** Ok, Jeremy Doe. It's Vanessa Calimag. Nice to meet you.
>
> **Jeremy:** Jeremy Lin, like the basketball player.

The basketball player? I was suddenly transported back in time to my days living in Pilsen just before I'd moved to the suburbs. I remembered that young basketball star whose story had made him an instant household name and whose marketing cohorts had coined the term "Linsanity." Most of all, I remembered I had promised the growing baby in my womb that he'd be "just like Jeremy Lin." Goosebumps came up all over my arms. *Did the universe really work this way?* Having already embarrassed myself for a second time in two days, though, I decided to keep that little tidbit to myself. I ended up googling him and found that he was on twitter and saw some photos of him and his sons. He was a dedicated dad; almost every photo he posted was with or about the kids.

The next day after work, I drove to the mediator's office with Zach in tow. "It's a big day for us, baby boy!" I told him as I was pulling into the parking lot. I was so excited to have closure coming on our divorce. As I parked in the lot, I noticed Dylan walking toward my car. I started to open my car door, and he opened it the rest of the way for me.

"Hey, can I help you guys upstairs?" he asked, smiling at me.

"For sure. Do you mind pulling Zach's car seat out? I'll grab the stroller from the trunk." Our last two meetings had been very amicable, and we'd made a lot of progress on our parenting schedule. I'd made some concessions on certain holidays, and so had he. I was finally coming to peace with where we were at. We both were. We walked toward the building and up the elevator together.

"He's been saying *mama* a lot when he's babbling. It's super cute."

"I know, right? I think he knows that's my name! I can't believe how quickly he's learning. He'll be saying *dada* soon too; I'm sure it's just a matter of days."

For the next two hours, we spoke with Marjorie, reviewing the last of the details of our parenting schedule and divorce decree. We'd gotten past the hard feelings somehow. I felt an energy of collaboration, and even a sense of trust, growing between us as she took her final notes. The divorce was, without a doubt, the best thing for Dylan and me, and we both knew it.

"Well, kids, it's been a pleasure," said Marjorie as she tapped the top of her legal pad, indicating she was done taking notes. "Your lawyers will take the last of my notes to draft the final documents, and you'll be able to complete your divorce in a matter of weeks. It's been an honor to get you through this process, and I've enjoyed watching you evolve your relationship into one that will show Zachary that you're committed co-parents."

"Thank you so much, Marjorie." I looked at Dylan and back at her. "I think I speak for both of us when I say that we could not have come this far without you. I can even tell you honestly that when I see Dylan, I no longer want to run him over with my car!" I laughed.

"Well, I appreciate that!" he said, joining me in the laugh.

Finally, Friday arrived. With the final round of mediation behind me, I felt the weight of the world had been lifted off my shoulders. Jeremy and I decided to have lunch at the same Thai restaurant as the week prior. As I walked through the revolving doors, I saw him waiting for me at the entrance. He was wearing the same black jacket, dark jeans, a navy-blue sweater, and a black baseball cap.

"Well, hello there!" I smiled at him and immediately closed the gap between us to hug him. We'd gotten so much closer in the past week, that I decided not to fight my affectionate nature.

"How did I get lucky enough to get a hug from you?"

"Why not?" I said, blushing. "Let's go in." I motioned toward the restaurant.

We sat down, this time at a table in the middle of the restaurant. Our conversation was lively, and we laughed over how we finally learned about each other's last names. After Jeremy had learned my last name, he'd found my photography website. He was pretty impressed with some of the images in my portfolio. An avid photographer too, he was asking about lighting setups, and I eagerly explained my approach and had many other stories about photography to share. I loved that we shared this passion. We also discovered we both worked out Lifetime Fitness (mine was in a nearby suburb called Skokie and his, of course, was in Algonquin). As we spoke, I appreciated him even more, and it crossed my mind that I could tell him what finding out his last name had meant to me but decided it was still a story for another day. When we'd finished lunch, Jeremy told me he had a gift for me. He reached into his pocket and handed me an envelope with a big smile on his face. I opened it up and found a gift card to Massage Envy.

"Well, you told me about your March Madness brackets, and I realized I needed to step up my game."

"So far, I'd say you're in the lead, Martial Arts Guy."

Jeremy walked me back towards my office again, and at the same spot as last time, we started parting ways.

"Are you going to work out this weekend?" he asked.

"Definitely."

"Mind if I tag along? I have my kids on Saturday, but I'm free on Sunday."

"It's a date then. I'll see you Sunday."

Chapter 13: Falling Together

I woke up on Saturday with a smile on my face as I heard Zach starting to stir in his crib. Nothing was more delicious to me than the sound of his voice. As I sat in the glider chair with my feet propped up in the ottoman nursing him that morning, I whispered, "You'll be with your daddy today, okay? Mommy's going to miss you. But I'll see you again in no time."

He grinned at me, drooling, his two front teeth starting to poke out from his gums. "Ma, ma, ma," he said proudly, tapping my shoulder with his hand.

"That's right; I'm your mama!"

Dylan wanted to pick up Zach before lunch and spend the afternoon with him. I'd planned my day accordingly, ready to spend an extra-long time at the gym, and then head to the mall to buy him an Easter outfit. Though I always missed my baby, I was learning to appreciate the 'me' time whenever I could get it. I got us ready for the day, daydreaming about how my date with Jeremy on Sunday would go, wishing I could see him today.

As I pulled into the parking lot at the gym after dropping off Zach, I noticed I had a text message from Jeremy saying his boys were with their mom, so perhaps we could see each other today. The universe again was conspiring to give me exactly what I wanted. I responded back that I'd love to see him.

I was relieved I'd brought a decent outfit to change into after working out. With him being only an hour away, I did a quick cardio workout and spent some time in the steam room, to ground myself in meditation before seeing him. I reflected on how grateful I was for reaching this point in my life. My heart was ready for love.

I put on a tight-fitting green top and a black cardigan that tied at the waist. Then I pulled up a pair of bootcut dark wash jeans and my favorite black boots. I felt confident. I was still working on the post-baby body, but this outfit was very flattering. I thanked my intuition for randomly pulling these exact pieces into my gym bag that morning, along with my makeup bag, which I didn't always carry around with me. I walked out to the parking lot to head out to my car, when a black Range Rover pulled up in front of me. Jeremy waved from the driver's side, and he rolled down the window. "Hop in!" he said with the big Jeremy smile that I had already memorized. Enthusiastically, I obliged. "Nice ride!" I said, as I slid into the front seat. I tossed my workout bag in the back. His car was immaculate. I wondered how in the world he could keep his car so clean with two young kids, and immediately hoped he wouldn't ask to see my car, which was a beat-up Honda Pilot that I certainly had not vacuumed out any time in recent memory. He was dressed in all black, also a 'Jeremy thing,' I had decided, and the same black baseball cap he'd worn on our first date.

We headed over to Old Orchard mall just down the road. "I haven't gotten the baby an Easter outfit yet, do you mind helping me find something?"

"Not a problem. I can find a few things for my boys too." He tapped his hand on the steering wheel to the beat of the song that was playing on the radio. It was nice seeing him in a different element. We made eye contact a few times on the short drive and he grinned at me. It was making my heart race! I hoped I'd have enough witty comments to last through our entire time together. We pulled into the parking garage by Macy's and got out. Coming in from the parking lot, we walked together closely, chatting comfortably. I wondered if he would try to hold my hand or put an arm around me, but noticed he was not making a move, playing it carefully. The one thing I'd forgotten to bring with me in my gym bag that day was my purse, so I was holding my wallet with a wrist strap awkwardly, which was perfect as I wasn't sure what to do with my hands anyway. After browsing around at a couple of places, we stopped into a Starbucks to sit and chat. He ordered a vanilla latte, and so did I, another one of the many things we were finding we had in common. The flow of our conversation was natural and lighthearted, and the chemistry was continuing to grow. After we walked out of the Starbucks, I started steering him in the direction of the store I wanted to go to.

"There's this store Janie and Jack I want to check out," I mentioned. "Let's head that way." I reached out for his hand, wondering what would happen. Our fingers interlocked. It felt like electricity was flowing between us.

At Janie and Jack, I found the outfit I wanted for Zach, a blue and green plaid shirt and navy pants that he would look adorable in, and had it rung up at the register. I noticed the time. "I have to leave soon. It's time to pick up Zachary." I looked at him, trying not to feel disappointed by our time coming to an end so soon. Jeremy squeezed my hand.

"I'll drive you back to your car." It felt nice to just feel his hand in mine. As we headed back towards Lifetime, I pointed out where my car was. As I reached into the back seat to grab my gym bag,

Jeremy took charge of the moment and said, "Go pick him up, meet me back at the mall, and we'll go from there."

Is he ready to meet my son? There was a certainty in his eyes that I couldn't dismiss. I paused for a moment, meeting his gaze. *Was I ready for him to meet my baby?* I squeezed his hand, every ounce of my intuition telling me I could trust this man.

"Okay. I'll text you when I'm on the way back." Though not a lot of words were exchanged, so much was said in that little conversation.

I rushed home to pick up my baby bag, including some baby food in case we stopped somewhere to eat. I also tidied up the house as best I could in case Jeremy ended up stopping by after the mall. My parents were in Ecuador, so we'd have the house to ourselves. My mind was racing a million miles a minute, wondering what was in store for the rest of the evening. Jeremy sent me a message:

> **Jeremy:** It might be a little chilly for the little guy to walk around. Do you want to just sit down at Cheesecake Factory?

It was like he read my mind. And he picked one of my favorite places! I told him I'd meet him there. I picked up Zachary from St. Martha's as usual and headed straight back to the mall, parking close to the restaurant on the north end of Old Orchard. By now, the sun was starting to set, and it was getting even chillier out. I had the baby zipped up snuggly in his coat and kissed his cheeks as I whispered in his ear about a special man named Jeremy Lin that he was about to meet. He was quiet, half asleep, and barely stirred as I got him out of the car. Setting his car seat safely in the stroller and putting a cover over it to protect him from the wind, I moved quickly to get us inside. We headed toward the elevators to get upstairs to the main dining area, and the doors slowly glided shut with only me and Zachary inside. I looked at the two of us in the reflection of the elevator doors as it brought us up one level. It had been just my baby and me as a pair for so long, and I was about to share my family unit with Jeremy. Much like the butterflies in my stomach on our first date, I felt my stomach swirling again. This time there was so much more on the line. Everything in me told me to keep going, and I felt an adrenaline rush flooding through me. The doors opened. I trusted my intuition and moved forward.

At the reception area, I spotted Jeremy quickly. Before I could properly introduce him to Zach, the hostess swept us away and brought us to our table. Without missing a beat, Jeremy helped me lift the stroller over a couple of stairs towards the back of the restaurant where we were being seated, and I set Zachary right next to me at the table. Jeremy took his seat across from me. As I got the baby situated, Jeremy pulled out a little plush rabbit that he'd bought for him while I was gone. "Thank you!" I exclaimed excitedly, truly surprised and grateful that he'd done something so sweet for Zach already. Still half asleep in the stroller, Zach yawned and stretched as he heard us talking. I tucked the plush rabbit into his hands and cooed at him as he continued to hang onto the last few moments of his nap. I was eager for him to wake up fully so I could properly introduce him to Jeremy.

We ordered our food, and Jeremy ordered us two glasses of wine, taking the liberty of choosing something for me – a cabernet, my favorite. I was impressed. The waitress promptly brought us our wine and my salad, but as I took my first bite, Zach started to whimper to let me know he was awake. I immediately snapped out of date mode and began to unstrap him from the stroller and to get ready to check his diaper. Jeremy intervened. "Can I hold him?" He asked eagerly. Without hesitation, I handed him over and

Jeremy smiled brightly at Zach and stood up. He paused to look at me and said, "You eat, I'll be right back." Off he went talking to Zachary excitedly, bouncing him gently and showing him around the dining room. He pointed up at a light fixture and then stopped to look at the plants in the restaurant, engaging him in conversation. He was a pro. My heart stood still as I watched him handle my son with ease and held back tears, thanking God for this miraculous moment. *This is what it feels like.* I was in awe of this man who seemed to care about me, now holding the most precious thing in my life and handling it like an absolute angel. After all these nights of writing down all the aspects of my perfect man, there he was in physical form, beaming at my child. I couldn't stop staring at him. The universe had delivered exactly what I asked for, and my heart overflowed with gratitude.

Suddenly, I remembered I had a plate full of food and a nice glass of wine in front of me. I smiled, relishing the opportunity to eat with both hands free. After a few minutes, Jeremy and Zach returned, and he happily bounced the baby on his lap while he ate his meal. We switched back and forth, holding Zachary as we enjoyed our time together. After dinner, it was fairly early, only 6 pm, so I asked Jeremy to follow me home. When we walked in, Rolo came dashing towards us to greet us and spent an extra-long time sniffing his new visitor.

"This is Rolo. Rolo meet Jeremy," I laughed. "I need to change Zach's diaper, but I should take Rolo out first…"

"I got it, I got it," he interrupted, moving quickly. "I'll take him for a walk. Go take care of the baby." Jeremy had already found Rolo's leash and was putting it around his neck. "I'll be back in a few minutes." I could not believe my eyes.

A few minutes later, Zach had a clean diaper, and Rolo was a happy camper with his new friend. I gave Jeremy a tour of our house, chatting with him about my life growing up in Morton Grove and in the city, and how much everything had changed since the baby arrived. I fed Zachary and nursed him, completely comfortable. Finally, I got Zach ready for bed upstairs, while Jeremy watched TV in the living room downstairs. In no time, Zach was asleep.

I walked back downstairs, and Jeremy was searching for a movie for us to watch. We settled on Argo, starring Ben Affleck, something neither of us had seen before. As the movie began, I was too distracted by the excitement of being near Jeremy and how it was making me feel. He rested his back against me as the opening scene came on. Almost instinctively, I cradled Jeremy's head in my hands, gently touching his ears as I tried unsuccessfully to focus on the movie. Ben Affleck was coming up with a crafty idea on how to extract six US nationals from Tehran, and I was wondering what it would feel like to kiss Jeremy. I hadn't had feelings like this surface in so long, and it was hard to control. Jeremy sat up and turned around to face me. Without saying a word, he leaned in to kiss me. A warm feeling ran through my entire body, and I wished this moment would never end. After all this time, I'd spent meditating on what love would feel like; it was surreal having it happen in the physical plane. But after a few minutes, his phone rang. It was his oldest son, Johan, who missed his daddy and wanted him to come home. While Jeremy was on the phone, I heard Zach start crying. He wasn't used to the sound of the new voice in the house. I went upstairs to get him, and as we returned downstairs, Jeremy was getting his jacket on ready to leave.

"I'm sorry, I can't stay."

"Don't worry; I completely get it. Daddy duty calls. Go take care of your kids."

Jeremy leaned in to kiss me goodbye. I closed the front door, my heart already aching to see him again, and I took Zach back upstairs and rocked him to sleep. I sat quietly in the glider, soaking in everything that had just happened.

My phone buzzed, and a message popped up from Jeremy:

> **Jeremy:** Well, now what? :) I miss you.
>
> **Me:** I miss you too. Don't text and drive!

I knew it was a long way home for him and wished he didn't live so far away. I almost had to pinch myself to remind me that today was real. Once I was sure the baby was sound asleep, I went downstairs to do some dishes and then started to get ready for bed. I felt my phone buzz again.

> **Jeremy:** Would it be too much for you if I came back after the boys are asleep? My mom is here, and they are fine through the night.
>
> **Me:** No, I don't mind!

About an hour later, he was back with a bag of takeout from one of his favorite restaurants near his home. I'd been so distracted I didn't realize how hungry I was until the smell of delicious seafood noodles were wafting through my house. We were certainly discovering that we had similar taste buds. We sat together in the kitchen talking and laughing. I showed him pictures of my family hanging in the sunroom, describing my siblings and each one of my nieces and nephews. I could see him trying to commit their names to memory, and he asked questions about what they were like. We tried watching a little more of the movie we'd started earlier, and we were about as focused on it as we were the first time. Laughing it off, we ended up cuddling on the couch until the early morning. Eventually I was starting to doze off with my head on his shoulder. "Do you want to go to sleep upstairs?" I asked him half asleep.

He looked at me seriously when he responded. "I don't want you to feel pressure to do anything, okay? I'm falling for you pretty hard, and more than anything, I want you to know I respect you. I'm not expecting anything to happen."

Our chemistry was undeniable, but I knew I wasn't ready for sex. Hearing him say those words made me feel even stronger about him. "I do trust you. I feel the same. I'm falling for you... I'm falling asleep, but I don't want you to leave yet. I'll miss you." He kissed me softly. It was already the middle of the night, and he had to be home early in the morning. We finally headed upstairs. Falling asleep next to this man I was falling in love with, felt as natural as breathing. Before I knew it, I could hear the alarm going off on his phone at 5 am. He got up to leave so he could be home for his children when they woke up.

Jeremy came back to see us the next afternoon. He brought Zach an iPod loaded up with Mickey Mouse cartoons so he could watch it while eating dinner. We went to dinner at a local diner in Morton Grove, and I watched Jeremy seamlessly carrying around my baby in the car seat. He propped him up right next to him in the booth when we sat down, feeding him a bottle of milk while we ate dinner. I was in awe of how well he could handle my son. It felt like a family. And yet there was so much to learn about him. He had two children that I hadn't met yet, a story leading up to this moment that I wanted to know more about. Sunday afternoon turned into Sunday evening and we both had to get back to work the next day. After spending most of the past 48 hours with Jeremy, our magical weekend was coming to a close. I didn't want it to be over.

Jeremy and I had talked openly about my master plan on Match.com and made more of a joke about it at the beginning of the weekend. I'd told him that I had intended to keep things light, as I had been through a lot and didn't know what I'd be ready for. Jeremy openly struggled with the idea of me meeting anyone else. While he wasn't outright pressuring me, he joked about texting each one of the guys I was talking to, to let them know they wouldn't be advancing to the next round. I played along, though I was very non-committal in my answers, shrugging it off and not confirming for him that I would actually be canceling my other dates.

After Jeremy left that evening, panic suddenly set in. *What if everything I was feeling this weekend was too good to be true?* My ego was holding onto the plan to meet other people, and yet when what I seemed to be looking for had appeared, so suddenly, it was hard for me to accept. I called Jeremy late that night.

"Hi babe," he said as he answered the phone. "Everything okay?"

"Hi there... I'm okay... I... well, I'm overwhelmed if I'm being honest. I had such an amazing time this weekend, and I wasn't expecting all this."

"I wasn't either honey; it was pretty incredible."

"I don't know how to say this, but I'm freaking out. My hands are shaking. I had this whole Match thing planned out, and there's a part of me wondering if I'm rushing into this and should just stick to my plan. I feel like I was swept into this whirlwind, and I'm afraid of making a mistake…"

He was silent for a minute, digesting what I'd just shared. "Listen, I get why you must be feeling this way. We just jumped into a lot in the past few days. After talking to you all this time, I know you have a good head on your shoulders, and I get why you made a plan like you did. I just can't help how I feel about you. Honestly, I don't like the idea of you meeting anyone else. I want you to trust *me* with your heart. But I can't force you into that either."

I was grateful he seemed to understand. "I know, and I'm sorry, I just didn't want to hide anything from you and let you know how I'm feeling right away. I guess I don't have any conclusions I'm drawing right now. It was a lot this weekend, you're right. I've never felt this way before. I think I just need to sleep on it…"

We hung up the phone a bit awkwardly, and I had a difficult time falling asleep, mulling over the fact that he didn't want me to meet anyone else. I wondered what my family would think of him, especially my sister, who was the most protective of me. I stared at the other side of the bed where Jeremy once was and hugged the pillow he had slept on, where the smell of him lingered faintly.

I woke up the next morning with this message on my phone.

> **Jeremy:** Dear Vanessa, I thought a lot about some of the hard stuff that came up last night, and I realized how important your process may be to you. If being unsure about us is always going to be in the back of your head due to not going on other dates, then I need you to do it. I don't want any impediment getting in the way of us getting closer someday because I think we could be really special.

Honestly, I've never met anyone like you, and
the times we have spent together have truly been
a joy. Hanging out with you and Z has been so
comfortable and relaxing. For my sake, I
probably should have tiptoed a little lighter
too, but it's been hard to control my feelings
for you. I just want to be with you all the
time.

Regardless I don't want a barrier between us
because the inherent climb with everyone
protecting you and being skeptical of me is going
to be challenging enough. So, go do your thing.
I'm not going to be able to really hear about
it, though. I mean, I have feelings and jealousy
like anyone else, but I'll tell myself to be a
big boy.

I'll be here waiting…

Jeremy

The next day at work, I could hardly concentrate. My lack of
decisiveness was frustrating to me, so I couldn't even imagine how
it was making Jeremy feel. I was in a battle with my heart and mind,
and I knew I was just trying to protect myself. After the weekend
I'd just had with him, I didn't feel like meeting anyone else. I buried
myself in the monotony of my spreadsheets, trying to zone out my
emotions for a few hours. On the way home that evening, I opened
up my laptop to check the profiles of the next dates I had lined up.
I clicked into my messages to see Jeremy's profile too. For some
reason I couldn't find it. His Match.com profile seemed to be
missing. I was confused. *Did he block me?*

In the peace and quiet of the train ride that had become a coveted
part of my day, I closed my eyes, put my hand over my heart, and
asked myself, "What does my heart say?" Listening to my heart had

gotten me through the worst of the divorce. I knew it wouldn't fail me now. As I sat there silently listening to my inner voice, I realized that the only thing standing in the way of my own happiness was my fear. I'd known for a long time exactly what I wanted out of a partner, and I'd manifested it into reality faster than I thought possible. I'd learned that finding a needle in a haystack was not impossible nor difficult, after all. All I had to do was become a magnet. I'd done the work from the inside out, and I'd found my perfect match. Instead of running away from my own happiness, I was going to run straight towards it, unapologetically. As if Jeremy knew I was thinking about him, my phone buzzed with a message from him as soon as I opened my eyes.

> **Jeremy:** Can we talk tonight?
>
> **Me:** Of course. How about 9? Zach will be asleep then.
>
> **Jeremy:** Okay, I'll give you a call.

My parents had come home from vacation while I was at work, and my dad was cooking up a storm when I got home. Though I had Jeremy on my mind all night, I wasn't ready to talk to my parents about him quite yet. They were happier than ever to see the baby again and tired from their trip. As soon as I'd put him down for the night, I felt my phone buzzing.

"Hey, you," I said softly as I started walking out of Zach's room.

"Hi babe."

"Perfect timing. The little guy just knocked out for the night."

"Oh, good. I miss that little man. How was your night with him?"

"It was great! He ate like a champion as usual. He was happy to have his grandma and grandpa back today. Hey, can I ask you something?"

"Sure."

"Did you block me on Match? I can't find your profile anymore."

He paused for a moment. "No, I took my profile down today."

"Interesting. Why did you do that?"

"I don't need it anymore. I found what I wanted." I got ready to explain my epiphany on the train this evening, but he jumped in before I could start. "Listen, I have something I need to say. I've been thinking about this all day. I know I said I'd be okay and to go do your thing. But I changed my mind. If you're with me, you should be with me. There's no room for anyone else in that equation. It doesn't work for me any other way. I know we joked about your March Madness brackets and it seems like fun and games. The thing is, I met your son. I spent the whole weekend falling for you. And I'm taking it seriously. I can't tread any lighter than I have been. I want you to be my girlfriend."

"Well, I'm glad you feel that way. What I wanted to tell you was, I spent the entire day thinking about you too. I don't want to meet anyone else. You're everything I've been looking for. You're the most incredible man I have ever met. I just want more time with you. There's so much more I want to know about you. I – "

"Well if you want more time together, why don't I come over then? You're officially my girlfriend and off the market, right?"

"That's exactly what I'm saying. You're my boyfriend, and *you* are off the market."

"I'm on the way then."

"Babe, my parents are home now, and they don't even know you exist yet... I can come outside and meet you, though," I said apologetically. There was no way I'd be able to bring him into the house at this hour.

"The drive to see you will be worth it. I'll call you when I pull up!"

Jeremy drove over to my house around 11:30 pm that evening. I slid past my parents, who'd both fallen asleep on the couch watching television and quietly opened the front door. I felt like a teenager, sneaking out this late at night. When I saw Jeremy standing next to his car in the street, I threw myself into his arms.

"Hi babe. I love you." I held nothing back and didn't intend to anymore.

"I love you too." He kissed my forehead and squeezed me.

We sat and talked in his car for a little while, and at midnight, he wished me a happy birthday. I had just turned thirty-four. I reflected back on last year's birthday with amazement at the way that life had turned completely around. Tiptoeing back into my house after midnight, I was as giddy as a teenager with a first love. My March Madness brackets had ended after the first date!

In the months that followed, we fell together. Once I relaxed into the knowing that I had found my soul mate, we wasted no time getting immersed in each other's lives. I invited Jeremy to Easter mass at St. Martha's, and he joined my entire family for brunch. Within the first few minutes of meeting my father, he seemed to have established trust and respect. I was floored. With a few raised eyebrows and just as many supportive friends, I was quickly integrating Jeremy into my everyday life. In a matter of days, Zach and I found ourselves seated at a table at a nice Brazilian steakhouse, meeting all of Jeremy's family at once: his mother, father, brother (and his new girlfriend), and most importantly, his two sons, Johan and Zakri. We were celebrating Johan's seventh birthday. When I saw Jeremy's children for the first time, they were both crying, having just woken up from a nap in the car. I saw Jeremy pick them both up, one in each arm, as they cried into his chest and he rocked back and forth to soothe them. My heart's energy shot across the room, and in that instant, I wanted to hold them too. These little boys looked so much like their daddy I could barely believe it. And they so clearly adored him; I was enamored by their dynamic immediately. Once the kids had calmed down and we got settled at our table, Jeremy told his kids, "Remember how I've been telling you about Ms. Vanessa? Can you say hi to her and her baby?"

"Hi," they both said in unison, a little shyly. Johan was the older of the two and seemed a lot more talkative. Zakri was tiny for a four-year-old, and true to his photos, his cheeks were chubby and adorable. I couldn't help myself from squeezing his face.

"Hi boys, I've heard so much about you! It's so nice to meet you finally! Johan, I've wanted to ask you something. I noticed you're missing some teeth. I wonder how much the tooth fairy gave you for those?"

He beamed at me, showing off his gummy smile. "These teeth were fifty dollars!" he exclaimed proudly. Meanwhile little Zakri asked to sit next to me and lisped in my ear about some of his favorite toys. I saw Johan and Zakri's eyes light up as I started feeding Zach his baby food. With my hands full entertaining the kids, Jeremy made sure I had food on my plate and ordered me a glass of red sangria. He squeezed my knee under the table every so often to remind me to eat something.

Everyone in Jeremy's family was wonderful. His mother, Joannie, was tag-teaming with me at dinner, trying to help me feed the baby as well as Zakri, who seemed to need the most help remembering we were here to eat; he was so busy playing with his Sonic plushy. She even offered to help me in the bathroom to help with diaper changing. She, too, was enamored with Zach. I felt like I had found my second family.

Johan and Zakri wanted to come along for the ride to bring Zach and me back home to Morton Grove, so all five of us got into Jeremy's Range Rover, which was now equipped with the base for Zach's car seat. It took me a moment to catch my breath as I realized this was going to be my new normal. This was the beginning of my beautiful family. Dylan had been supportive when I told him I'd met someone new, and he had also started dating someone. Things had really fallen together for all of us.

Johan and Zakri were thrilled to have Zach sitting in between them and were playing with him the entire ride home. As we got onto the expressway, Jeremy turned up the radio to an upbeat pop song that I'd never heard before. "Zakri, it's your song! Let's sing it!" Jeremy started tapping his hand on the gearshift and I looked at him curiously. I'd missed the boat on all of the music from the past year. Little Zakri started bobbing his head perfectly to the beat of the song, and suddenly both of them were singing their hearts out.

You're insecure, don't know what for
You're turning heads when you walk through the do-o-or
Don't need makeup to cover up
Being the way that you are is eno-o-ough

Everyone else in the room can see it
Everyone else but you

Baby, you light up my world like nobody else
The way that you flip your hair gets me overwhelmed
But when you smile at the ground, it ain't hard to tell
You don't know, oh, oh, you don't know you're beautiful...

Jeremy looked at me and gave me a wink as he kept singing along. I couldn't have fallen harder than I did at that moment. As we pulled into the driveway at my parents' house, all of them got out of the car to walk us to the front door. Before Zach and I turned to go inside, I gave them each a hug. Johan and Zakri kissed Zach on the cheek.

"See you soon my sweeties! Baby Zach and I will see you next weekend, okay?"

I leaned in close to Jeremy and whispered in his ear. "I love you like crazy. Thanks for today. Call me later?" I kissed him on the cheek and brought the baby inside.

Chapter 14: Moving Out

Boxes lined the walls of our tiny apartment. This was the place we'd called home for the past two years. The air conditioning unit was turned all the way up on this hot July day, and I listened to its hum as I carefully packed away my books and our children's toys. Jeremy was downstairs, loading the moving truck. He'd taken care of all the big things in the apartment, and I was doing cleanup on the little things in the living room. He had rolled up the worn-out practice jiu-jitsu mat we'd used to line our living room floor and makeshift play area. It was the same spot that the kids had used to wrestle, have impromptu dance parties, and lie down to rest while we watched movies — the same place where we would inflate air mattresses at night for Johan and Zakri to sleep on. Zach (whom we soon nicknamed "Bubba") had his crib set up next to our bed in the bedroom, which left us just enough room to set up dresser drawers for some of our clothes. Bubba loved his brothers intensely and had no recollection of a time without them in his life. I called them the three musketeers. There was a lot of life lived in these seven hundred square feet; every inch of it well worn. When we had picked this place, it was a matter of practicality; our kids were young, did not require much space, and we were very literally starting over again with our finances. A small, one-bedroom apartment seemed to make the most sense as we started to plan the rest of our lives together. It was the happiest time of my life.

My hands were swollen, and my back was aching as I cleared away books from the shelf, finding small pieces of leftover Legos from the children's vast number of creations over the years. On the wall behind where our couch had been, I found Star Wars stickers secretly placed. Carefully, I peeled Yoda and R2D2 off the paint. My hands were going numb, the first signs of carpal tunnel – quite normal in pregnancies as my doctor had told me. Hunched over, my right hand braced my aching lower back.

I surveyed the nearly empty living room. This tiny apartment had held my heart and blown it wide open. It radiated with growing love and the physical manifestation of my dreams coming true. Mementos of our beach wedding in Puerto Rico had been carefully wrapped and tucked into moving crates, and I was excited to imagine where those pieces would go in our new house in Skokie, just a town over from where my parents lived. Remnants of our summer trips to Disney World, baseball games, and ski trips to Colorado were also packed away. I stumbled upon some ultrasound images that had been tucked in between books on the shelf. Six months prior, when I'd gone to the ER, completely nauseous and dehydrated, they'd given me an ultrasound, and I saw the little life growing inside of me. "I'm not quite sure what I see here," I mentioned.

"Yes, of course, let me show you," the technician responded. "It's really early. You're only about six weeks pregnant, so there's not much you can make out. But there's a little heart right here!" she pointed to a dot in the center of the screen that at first I could not distinguish from the other grainy dots that made up the rest of the image. As I squinted, I noticed it making the tiniest movement. A heart was beating. It took my breath away, and I started to tear up. As she shifted the ultrasound around, she turned up the volume so we could hear the sound of the tiny little heartbeat.

"Listen to that. Do you hear it? It's incredible!" Jeremy said with one hand resting on top of his head in wonder. He beamed down at me, holding my hand as I laid the hospital bed.

"Oh, that little peanut! He or she is making me so sick!" I said, though I was feeling slightly better now that I'd had some fluids put into me.

As we got ready to leave, the technician handed me three grainy black and white images that had just printed out of the machine. I stared at them, feeling some sense of familiarity with this moment that I couldn't place my finger on.

"As far as we can tell, so far, so good. Everything is working out," she said with a smile. She whisked her way out of the room, needing to move onto the next patient. Suddenly, I remembered the dream I'd had years ago, where Sonia had shown me proof that everything was working out for me. I finally understood what she had meant.

Three weeks after the ultrasound, Jeremy had found a new housing development where he wanted us to build our home, and he'd put down the deposit. "We're going for it, babe. Let's build our dream home!" he said as he showed me the paperwork, his eyes lit up like it was Christmas day.

Our life together was evolving at a lightning pace, and I loved where our journey was taking us. We were worlds away from the time where our closest friends and family members were questioning how fast things were going and whether we knew what in the world we were doing. We'd laughed it off and continued living our lives full out. Eventually, everyone had come around and warmed up to the idea of us becoming an instant family. We'd gotten engaged about four months after we met when Jeremy swept me up on a trip to Belize and, at the end of a pier, had gotten down on one knee and asked me to be his wife. Without hesitation, I said yes. Nine months later, we were married.

Just before our wedding, I told him about the story of Jeremy Lin, the basketball player whose story I'd watched on television when my life was unraveling.

"I promised Bubba when he was still in my belly that he'd be just like Jeremy Lin. I had no idea I'd get such a literal answer from the universe."

He looked at me, wide-eyed, and I thought I might be moving him to tears. He pulled me closer and kissed me softly. I tucked my head onto his chest, and then I felt him shaking. When I looked up at him, he was laughing. "I can't believe you wished for a Jeremy Lin."

"Of course, I did. I'm really brilliant at manifesting what I want in case you haven't noticed." I kissed his cheek and pulled a throw blanket over my feet at the end of the couch. Our couch. As we were starting our humble beginnings from scratch, we'd also started a new collection of our own furniture. With that very couch now safely loaded into the moving truck, Jeremy came back upstairs, his head in a full sweat.

"Almost done, babe?" He wiped the side of his face with his t-shirt.

"Yes, honey. I couldn't reach a few of the dishes on the top shelf in the kitchen, but other than that, we're all set."

"Okay, I'll take care of it. I'll bring all these down first." He motioned to the boxes I'd lined up against the wall.

"Thanks. I need to make a quick call. I promised Heidi I'd check in on her. She's got that big presentation with our client today." One of the many benefits of having Jeremy as my partner was that he understood my passion for my work. He encouraged me to push myself harder and to think like a business owner, and so he never took offense to me taking work calls on a moment's notice. It was no accident that after just a few months of knowing him, my career began to flourish. We were able to manage a schedule for our kids that allowed me to travel frequently, and before I knew it, my career was back in full swing, and I was on the way to yet another promotion. I was able to build the team that I'd always wanted, and I traveled all over the world, helping build solutions for our clients. Life was brimming with promise in every direction.

One of my business trips had taken me to Tokyo, where I'd had a chance to learn a bit about Japanese culture, and the beautiful art of Kintsugi. In this tradition, imperfections and breaks in pottery are celebrated and honored, using a lacquer dusted with powdered gold to repair and glue pieces together, making the piece even more beautiful and stronger than it was before. The symbolism it held for me was profound, and I liked to think of my life as a work of Kintsugi. From the time my life fell apart until it came back together again, I learned that on the other side of fear, sorrow, and grief, was absolute bliss, satisfaction, and love. I learned that gathering the pieces of my life was an essential part of opening myself up to a new me that was wiser, braver, and readier to accept the magic I had inside of me all along. I had learned to dance with the universe, to conspire with it, and to trust that everything would work out beautifully.

By the time I'd finished my call, Jeremy had finished moving all the boxes I'd just packed downstairs. "Hey, let's take a quick picture. I want to send a photo to the boys so they can see what the apartment looks like completely empty!" He propped his phone up on the kitchen counter as I stood in the middle of the living room. Setting a timer, he ran over to me and stood behind me with his hands around my waist, holding my growing belly. In just three months, life would once again be changing in a major way. Girl or boy, we were not sure, and decided it would be another one of life's great surprises.

And so, on that last day in our tiny apartment, my swollen fingers stumbling clumsily across the nearly packed boxes, with an aching back and tiny legs kicking the inside of my belly, I stood in awe of the life I'd created with my husband and children. My heart overflowed with gratitude at my unbelievable fortune. Across the room, Jeremy was packing up what little remained in our kitchen. Slowly, I walked over to him, rested my head on his chest, as I had become accustomed to, and he kissed my forehead. I smiled contentedly and took a deep breath. The little life inside me stirred happily. Exhaling, I made space in my heart for the next miraculous adventure to begin.

www.ingramcontent.com/pod-product-compliance
Lightning Source LLC
Chambersburg PA
CBHW022005090426

42741CB00007B/905